Transforming Conflict

Transforming Conflict

The Blessings of Congregational Turmoil

By Terasa Cooley

An Alban Institute Book

ROWMAN & LITTLEFIELD
Lanham • Boulder • New York • London

Published by Rowman & Littlefield
An imprint of The Rowman & Littlefield Publishing Group, Inc.
4501 Forbes Boulevard, Suite 200, Lanham, Maryland 20706
www.rowman.com

86-90 Paul Street, London EC2A 4NE

British Library Cataloguing in Publication Information Available

Library of Congress Cataloging-in-Publication Data

Names: Cooley, Terasa, author.
Title: Transforming conflict : the blessings of congregational turmoil / by
  Terasa Cooley.
Description: Lanham : Rowman & Littlefield, 2022. | Includes
  bibliographical references and index.
Identifiers: LCCN 2021061802 (print) | LCCN 2021061803 (ebook) | ISBN
  9781538161821 (cloth) | ISBN 9781538161838 (paperback) | ISBN
  9781538161845 (ebook)
Subjects: LCSH: Conflict management—Religious aspects—Christianity. |
  Church controversies.
Classification: LCC BV4597.53.C58 C67 2022 (print) | LCC BV4597.53.C58
  (ebook) | DDC 250—dc23/eng/20220304
LC record available at https://lccn.loc.gov/2021061802
LC ebook record available at https://lccn.loc.gov/2021061803

Contents

Foreword

This is a good book. It is an important book. That's why I have a problem. My problem is that people may not pick up this book unless they have a problem—or more specifically, a problem in their congregation. As a lifetime inhabitant of congregations, and as a well-seasoned consultant and teacher in congregations, I know the pattern. Differences, both large and small, are a part of the very fabric of all congregations, of all communities. In addition, many—if not most—congregations (persons, families, communities) have experienced some level of trauma. When traumas intrude and when differences of preference, practice, or opinion rub up against one another sufficiently to create discomforting heat, the congregation turns to the leader to "fix it." When the fix is not forthcoming, the differences deepen and people feel like they have to "do something." One of the things people do at such a time is search for resources to help them with their problem. That's my problem. That is the time people will most likely pick up this book.

This book is not about how to *fix* something. It is about how to *be* something. That "something" includes how to be more fully the person you can be, how to live in community with others who see things differently from you, how to live out the faith and values that you espouse and hold dear, how to be more healthy in mind, spirit, and relationships. My problem is that people will read this book because they will think it is about fixing an uncomfortable situation in their congregation, and they will read with the hope of returning to a state of congregational comfort. There is so much more here.

Let's start with conflict and its ever-present partner, change. Conflict is not a problem (and Terasa will more than once in this book identify it as an opportunity). I have long favored the definition of conflict as two or more ideas in the same place at the same time. Conflict doesn't always have to create heat and discomfort. At its most basic level, conflict is part of the engine that drives us. Without conflict we would only have one idea or one set of experiences. We would only do what we've always done. We would only know what we already understand. That is not a condition of comfort; it is stagnation. Stagnation in a steadily changing world is death. We should be careful about any search for congregational comfort that we pursue.

I recently worked on some writing to support a series of ongoing conversations with some denominational leaders. I was making the case that we are at a transitive moment in our North American culture when our values and our behaviors are changing in ways that no currently living generation has experienced before—an epochal change. At one point I wrote: "This epochal change is written about incessantly and the evidence of death/new birth is continuously catalogued: a pandemic and post-pandemic deep shift; a rising global populism spawning a historic political divide between the wealthy and the poor that has eviscerated the middle class; a shift in the holding and use of power underwritten by changes in technology and communication; mercurial shifts in international agreements and relationships that undermine global stability and security; a climate change crisis that resides quietly beneath all other challenges with deadly global consequences." Can you imagine such a sentence? And, it's not even complete. Each of us can add our own symptoms and evidence of cultural disruption from what seems to be an unending stream of changes.

If such disruptions are continuous at the global, national, and community levels, how could any of us hope to live comfortably and not engage others who have different ideas, different experiences, different needs and wants? To seek to fix, resolve, or manage conflict in such a setting is naive. The sentiments of fixing, resolving, and managing lead us to a nostalgia for a remembered or manufactured past that we cannot return to, cannot recapture. Conflict must be transformed; we must understand its healthy capacity to transform us.

In her work with congregations in conflict, it is significant that Terasa doesn't offer help to change our congregations to meet our own ideas or needs, nor does she encourage us with tools to change or manage others who disagree with us. Instead, she offers a book about changing ourselves. The self, after all, is the only place where we actually have control in a world and in communities continuously confronted by swift, deep, and global change. While this book will be of help to leaders in congregations experiencing conflict, it's value is in helping each of us learn how to live healthily in a world and in communities where the tension of conflict cannot be avoided. If thoughtfully embraced, conflict can be transformative.

This leads to my second consideration. People who choose to be a part of a faith community—a congregation—should expect to be transformed. In many religious traditions this is referred to as formation. We introduce our children to faith through sabbath schools, youth groups, camps, and conferences with the wish that they be formed in faith and that by such formation they will be guided in their self-understanding, their choices, and their relationships. But by signing up with a congregation, we are also submitting ourselves to formation as adults. In my own United Methodist tradition, we speak of this formation as discipleship. Discipleship is built on disciplines—practices that provide insight and shape to both our understanding and our actions. The mission statement of my denomination is to "make disciples of Jesus Christ for the transformation of the world." Whatever some may think of our track record, we are at least bold enough to rightly state that we are interested in disciples (changed individuals) and the transformation of the world (changed communities). It is a purpose of faith to transform us. If we experience conflict in our congregation, is it not right to expect that conflict experienced in the context of faith should transform both us and our congregation? Conflict transformation is not about wrestling order out of chaos. It is certainly not about returning to the time and state that we knew before the conflict. Conflict transformation is about forming ourselves and shaping our congregations so that faith can bring meaning to the differences and changes that are unavoidably constant and deep in our lives.

This brings me to my final concern, which is about community. Terasa's book on conflict transformation begins with understanding and shaping ourselves. This is right and true because the only real locus of control for any of us is the self. But then she moves from "me" to "we," from the healthy self to healthy communities. Healthy communities are both critical to and essential in a global and national time when we experience institutional gridlock in the midst of deep yet quicksilver change. Gridlock in our national politics and in our global corporate economics means that any real change must come from the local level—from the community, and from individuals willing to be in community with one another for a healthy purpose. And it is at the community level that we will build the stability needed to withstand the speed of change that overwhelms us individually. I am fascinated by the Polish sociologist Zygmunt Bauman, who calls our time a "liquid culture." By liquid culture Bauman means a world changing so quickly that the time necessary for a reasoned response is disallowed. By the time a response to any change is determined and moved toward implementation, the conditions requiring the response will have changed yet again.

None of us could ever manage such a world by ourselves. But to be in community means to open ourselves to the differences and discomforts of relationships with others. This is why our biblical texts, translators, and interpreters speak to us about covenant communities. This is why New Testament commentators and teachers settle so quickly on the theme of messianic community as a way of understanding the teachings of Jesus and the letters of Paul. If our texts and traditions give us a way of personal living, they also give us a way of living with one another. To be fully ourselves, we need to live in healthy community. To help form healthy communities, we need to risk being fully ourselves. We need the formation of faith to be both self and community.

Biblical theologian Walter Brueggemann has been very instructive to me, pointing out that each time the Israel of the Hebrew Bible had to confront the disordering of its world (such as the Exodus and the Exile), the people had to answer the same two questions again and again: How will we now be with God? and, How will we now be with one another? It is the second question that is the question of community. Now that we live in a liquid culture, a world divided by populism, a nation that will not release itself from its debilitating myths of racism and homophobia—how will we now be with one another? A really good faith question never really goes away. The same questions that ancient Israel needed to address in its own dislocations are before us now in our own chaotic time.

Transforming conflict is not about escaping it. It is not about fully resolving differences, and certainly not about capturing happiness (personal comfort) in our congregations. Learning to live in a world marvelously but frighteningly powered by the tensions and differences that produce conflict is about not being trapped by our own instinctive natures. It is about being more fully formed by our own faith aspirations and practices, and about seeking how we can be with one another in a healthy and life-giving way. Here, Terasa offers steps down that better path. Thanks be to God.

Gil Rendle
Author of *Quietly Courageous: Leading the Church in a Changing World*
October 12, 2021

Introduction

I am one of those odd people who doesn't mind conflict. In fact, I kind of enjoy it—*when done well.* I prefer to get to the heart of things. Nothing irritates me more than to feel like something important is being unsaid or hidden. I prefer a challenging exchange to a cheap peace.

I was just 23 years old when I started my ministerial preparation. My denominational process at the time required aspiring ministers to be evaluated by a psychiatrist for our fitness for ministry (a daunting prospect!). After a battery of tests, including the infamous Rorschach test (it seemed all bats and butterflies to me), the psychiatrist declared me fit and said: "You are remarkably equipped to deal with high levels of conflict." I told a friend of mine about this, admittedly with some pride, and my friend said, "You know, Terasa, not everyone would think that is a compliment!"

Having said this, I admit that even to this day, I still get anything from butterflies to alligators in the pit of my stomach when faced with the prospect of a difficult conversation or having to confront someone. I don't like to needlessly upset others or be misunderstood or disliked for my efforts. But I have always felt that my way through that discomfort lay in facing it head on and not avoiding it.

Facing it head on, however, has many different interpretations! It has taken me years to learn not to crash in but to hold steady, to be clear and honest without blaming and shaming. I know I sometimes still stumble and err on one side or the other. But learning how to creatively and openly work through conflict has benefited me more in ministry (and life) than any other acquired skill.

A large part of what I had to work through was an unfortunate tendency to try to *fix things*—a common trait among ministers, but I had it in abundance. As someone who is an "8" on the Enneagram personality style profile (variously named the "Challenger," the "Protector," or the "Hero"—you get the idea without even knowing much about the Enneagram), I love nothing more than stepping in on behalf of the underdog and using my considerable power of persuasion to make things right and just. Certainly, it is important to sometimes use one's power to be an ally or to challenge an unjust system, but in interpersonal conflicts, the truth is that *it doesn't work*. It is almost impossible to solve someone's problems for them.

I'll explain this more in the chapter on systems, but for the moment let me say that the most life- and faith-affirming moments in my ministry have been when I have learned how to *get out of the way*, to lay the groundwork for conversations where everyone gets to speak their truth and everyone learns something new (most especially me).

I realize that many people are not like me. For some, conflict is not something to embrace but instead is something that petrifies. I honor that response and understand why. But I believe that today's world requires all of us to learn new ways of being in relationship to one another that is not just yelling over the fence at each other or running fast the other way.

The skills that I have learned in conflict transformation are not skills that are taught by our wider culture. We didn't have classes in high school that helped us understand nonviolent communication (wouldn't it be great if we did!). But I believe these are necessary skills to help move us toward a way not just to coexist, but to constantly learn and grow within ourselves and in relation to others.

Therefore, the goals of this book are:

- To help us better understand how our own minds and bodies respond to conflict and to learn how to teach our minds and bodies a new way of responding.
- To develop skills for responding to conflict in relationships in a more healthy and productive manner.

- To understand the cycles of conflict and systems in congregational life.
- To develop congregational practices in which conflict can be treated as an opportunity for growth rather than a crisis of division.

There is a kind of progression in this book that begins with the individual development of self-awareness, then moves to how we take that awareness into our interactions with others and learn skills for healthy conversations, and then ultimately look at congregational dynamics as a whole system that must be navigated.

To some degree, this is a false construct. We can never really know ourselves as an independent self, outside of our relationships and community; our interactions with one another are not just one-on-one conversations, but carry the weight of conversations that have come before and the concentric circles of conversations that move outward. Congregational life is not just a murky system without clear players in it. Nevertheless, I think it helps to address these categories as interrelated but also discrete, for each requires skill sets that build on one another.

Where better to learn skills at all of these levels than in a religious community? If we can create the kind of community that helps us grow in self-awareness, that holds us in love in the midst of our pain and distress, and that helps us walk together toward a new way, this indeed becomes a noble mission. This is not just about figuring out how we can all just get along. It is about learning how a congregation can build the skills within itself in order to meet its mission to serve the world in a new way.

This book includes exercises and discussion questions to help your congregation process the work together, though these can also be used for individual enlightenment.

I do want to note at this point that many of the practices and recommendations of typical nonviolent communication make a certain presumption of an equity of power among the participants. That works fine if there is cultural hegemony in the group. But ultimately, we must recognize that certain cultures carry more weight than others, and that many congregations continue to be steeped in the hegemony of White culture, making it difficult for people of other identities and cultural backgrounds to feel that they can participate in congregational systems with the same level of privilege assumed by Whites. If power is significantly unbalanced, then real harm can occur when people in more vulnerable positions are expected to engage in practices that make them even more vulnerable. I will address these concerns more specifically in different parts of the book, as well as in a special chapter, but I want to acknowledge this deficit from the beginning. I am still learning how to apply my growing understanding of the reality of White supremacy to congregational life. It is always an unfolding journey.

It is also important in the beginning to identify a difficult and delicate balance that occurs when we seem to be asserting that people must always take responsibility for their own part in a conflict. As noted above, there are often power imbalances in conflict, and people have been abused by those power imbalances. One cannot assume that, through the methods I will outline, an abusive person will come to see the error of their ways. Demanding that each party look at their own role in a conflict can often result in blaming the victim, rather than giving responsibility to the abuser. And yet, there is a reason why survivors of abuse reject the label of "victim." Being able to take some responsibility, *not for the abuse*, but for the ability to learn something from the experience, can be empowering in and of itself.

It is also possible for people to hide behind the label of "victim" and thereby miss the opportunity for change. In her challenging book, *Conflict Is Not Abuse*, Sarah Schulman takes an unflinching look at how to distinguish between real harm and avoidance:

> [A]t many levels of human interaction there is the opportunity to conflate discomfort with threat, to mistake internal anxiety for exterior danger, and in turn to escalate rather than resolve . . . this dynamic, whether between two individuals, between groups of people, between governments and civilians, or between nations is a fundamental opportunity for either tragedy or peace. Conscious awareness of these political and emotional mechanisms gives us all a chance to face ourselves, to achieve recognition and understanding in order to avoid escalation towards unnecessary pain.[1]

Again, it is delicate work to determine the difference between self-protection and avoidance, and we should always find help in identifying that balance as our own perspective may not be sufficient.

Change inevitably begets conflict, as there are as many ways of processing change as people. And in times of enormous change the conflicts can be commensurately large and, sometimes, as terrifying as the changes. As this book is being written we are still in the midst of the pandemic reality, when congregations have been forced to dramatically change at a moment's notice, and there is no sign of when the pandemic will completely end, if ever. It is clear that an "old normal" will not be regained, and just as apparent that our "new normal" has yet to be defined.

As I will discuss more fully in chapter 1, in recent years congregations have been called upon to make many significant changes to help reverse the tide that leads people away from organized religious life. And yet, in order to make such changes, we will inevitably expose deep conflicts about what is most important to retain in congregational life. At times like this, it is even more essential for people to have tools for addressing conflict in a healthy and open way, creating an even greater opportunity for true transformation to take root.

I write as a minister deeply rooted in the Unitarian Universalist tradition, and therefore much of my experience takes place within that context. But I believe that congregational life is congregational life and, no matter the polity, conflict within community takes some universal forms. My hope is that religious leaders—both lay and professional, from any denomination or tradition—may find these reflections and tools useful.

There is already a great deal of literature addressing conflict in congregations, much of which has been helpful to me in my developing understanding of conflict. I will discuss different methodologies more explicitly in the first chapter, but I believe that the focus on the *transformational opportunity* of conflict, as well as deeply examining the mind/body manifestations of conflict, mark this book as unique.

In this book I will utilize stories of conflicts that I have personally experienced or that I have been told by colleagues of several denominations. Most of them have been altered in some ways to protect the confidentiality of the congregation, and some are amalgams of several stories. All are told not to point out errors made by individuals or churches, but in the hope that you can recognize your own experience in these stories and to consequently learn from them.

So, I invite you to take a deep breath, let go of your anxiety as much as possible, and join me in this journey.

Part I

UNDERSTANDING THE NATURE OF CONFLICT

Chapter One

A New Way of Looking at Conflict

Why "Transformation"?

> Deep conflicts are stressful and painful. At worst, they are violent and destructive. Yet at the same time, they create some of the most intense spiritual encounters we experience. Conflict opens a path, a holy path, toward revelation and reconciliation.
>
> —John Paul Lederach[1]

When I tell people outside of congregational life that I help congregations work through conflict, this is often met with surprise: "There are conflicts in churches?" I suppose that if you're unfamiliar with how congregations usually operate, there's an expectation that we have created a kind of heaven on earth, with everyone floating peacefully together.

Anyone who has spent any time in a congregation knows that such an Eden does not exist! Even the most healthy and dynamic congregations experience conflict *all the time*. And why wouldn't that be true? In a congregation we bring our deepest values, our most vulnerable hurts, and our most tender aspirations. Given that these are all deeply individual feelings, it is almost a necessity that they would collide with one another at some point. John Paul Lederach says, "To speak well and to listen carefully is no easy task at times of high emotions and deep conflict. People's very identity is under threat."[2]

Given this reality of the necessity of conflict in congregations, how can we respond to it? Why is it so scary and painful? And what do we do about it?

First, we must accept that the evidence of conflict *doesn't mean we have done something wrong. It means we have something we need to learn.*

Second, we must realize that if we feel ill-equipped to deal with conflict, it isn't because we are bad, or needlessly afraid. It is because our western, White culture does little to teach us the skills of addressing conflict.

I'm not talking about simple disagreements of fact here. Disagreement is not the same thing as conflict. Conflict is when we feel deeply at odds with one another, or misunderstood in a significant way. As I'll discuss in the next chapter, there is a deep, biological reason why conflict makes us feel afraid. Something that feels like a threat to our identity, to our relationships, to our way of understanding the world, to the values we hold most dear, is bound to be a shock to us—not just on the surface, but deep in our bodies.

It may seem that I'm talking contradictions here: Conflict is healthy! Conflict is terrifying! Well . . . yes. As F. Scott Fitzgerald famously said, "The test of a first-rate intelligence is the ability to hold two opposed ideas in the mind at the same time, and still retain the ability to function."³ Or, I put it slightly differently: wisdom is the ability to understand two inherently contradictory ideas and know that both of them are true. Not an easy task in a world in which most people want to choose between and either/or. I often say that one of my personal disciplines is to try to remember to say "and" rather than "but."

HOW IS CONFLICT TRANSFORMATION DIFFERENT?

One way of addressing conflict that many of us are familiar with is *conflict mediation*. Mediation usually involves a disinterested, or at least unbiased, facilitator who helps hold a healthy space for people to talk through their disagreements. They do not "fix" a problem so much as create and enforce guidelines for a less heated conversation. It is most helpful if employed early on, before things escalate too severely. Mediation is incredibly helpful and necessary at times—at least people can be in the same room and talk with less harm. But in a congregational setting where it may be difficult to find someone who is "disinterested," it can only take things so far. When it comes to deeper emotional and value-laden differences mediation may be helpful, but it is insufficient.

Another well-known process is *conflict resolution.* This is usually the result of a successful mediation, and typically involves reconciling something objective that is of value to both parties. The tools of compromise and negotiation can help each party feel that they have at least received something that they were hoping for. The idea of "resolution" is that the dispute has ended, and people can move on. But again, in a congregational setting, the disputes are rarely about something objective, except as proxies for an emotional issue that can never be fully resolved. King Solomon understood this well! Just as we cannot divide a baby to make two parties happy, we cannot split our values into two.

Conflict transformation has something different, or something more robust, than peace or resolution in mind. *Transformation* utilizes the conflict to create an opportunity (yes, opportunity!) for everyone involved to grow and to learn and come back together changed as a result.

Conflict transformation has its roots in many traditions; in fact, every religious tradition has its own form of it. But as a well-articulated theory, it grows out of the work of John Paul Lederach and other Mennonite scholars and practitioners. Lederach has served as a peace negotiator in highly conflicted places such as Northern Ireland, Colombia, and South Africa. The truth and reconciliation process that helped transform South Africa is an example of this process. For Lederach, peace is not an abstract or fuzzy concept. It is a living, breathing possibility that is never completely fulfilled, but always possible.

Lederach defines it this way:

> Conflict transformation is to envision and respond to the ebb and flow of social conflict as life-giving opportunities for creating constructive change processes that reduce violence, increase justice in direct interaction and social structures, and respond to real-life problems in human relationships.[4]

That's a complicated sentence, so let's break it down a little. "To envision" tells us that we have to set aside our stuck positions and imagine something different that each of us can learn from conflict. "Constructive change" offers the possibility that together we can build a new understanding and way of being together. "The ebb and flow of social conflict" acknowledges the reality that conflict will always be there—we will never get to a place of complete peace, but we can enter into a dynamic and adaptive way of exploring how we can be together differently. "Increase justice" leads us, as Martin Luther King Jr. famously said, to the realization that "without justice, there can be no peace." For Lederach, conflict is not a problem, but an opportunity for spiritual growth, as referenced above: "Conflict opens a path, a holy path, toward revelation and reconciliation."[5]

I was trained in this methodology (which we will unpack in depth in subsequent chapters) during my doctoral work at Hartford Seminary, by one of Lederach's students. I found it intriguing and exciting . . . and then I promptly forgot about it when I began my work as a district executive—a role that required me to assist congregations in times of conflict. And conflict there was! Hoo boy! When I arrived in the district there were six congregations in deep levels of entrenched conflict.

In one of these congregations, I was told that ushers would greet newcomers at the door with a friendly: "Welcome to our church, we hate our minister!" There was a deep division between the music director and the minister, and everyone felt like they had to take sides. Using the method of working with conflict that was popular at the time, I interviewed almost all of the major players and produced a report naming the issues with some recommendations included. I held a meeting of said players to present this report, thinking they would appreciate my insight. Instead, the meeting concluded with people yelling at one another, yet again, and many walking out. Not exactly a success!

In another congregation, a minister and board needed to confront a music director who was undermining the minister's and board's authority and pilfering from the music accounts. After many meetings with the music director, it became clear that she was not going to change her ways and, indeed, didn't see any problems with what she had done. The board was forced to terminate her employment. But as frustrating as she was to church leadership, she was beloved by the choir! A firestorm of fury with the board erupted. Given the employment laws of the state, the board could not reveal the details of why the music director was dismissed, so board members felt hamstrung in any conversations. I had the bright idea of convening a congregational meeting in which the board as a whole and the lawyer involved could try to explain as best they could what had happened. Instead of creating clarity, this meeting also devolved into chaos and heated rhetoric. In one case a congregant came up to confront the board, and was so consumed with anger he was literally spitting. As I was standing close by, I unfortunately received the results of his anger! Being spit upon was definitely a low point in my career.

After a year or so of recognizing the futility of these approaches, I finally remembered my training in conflict transformation. I shifted my approach, and instead of trying to intervene, I conducted training to help teach congregations—leaders and individuals—how to develop the skills and processes to do their *own* work in addressing their conflicts. Within a few years, major conflicts that had exploded into needing intervention were relatively uncommon. This was not due entirely to my work with congregations, but I believe that having both clergy and lay leaders trained in a new way to approach the work made a big difference.

As I said in my introduction, this kind of training can have an impact on a number of levels: First, to help individuals develop their own capacity for growth. Second, to create opportunities and processes for people to address their conflicts with and between one another. And third, and I believe most important, to develop healthy congregational patterns of working with conflict that will ultimately help people fulfill their congregational mission, which is, of course, the deeper purpose of congregations.

THE PURPOSE OF THE CHURCH

I often will provocatively say that "the purpose of the church is not to make people happy!" This is wisdom learned from the work of congregational consultant Gil Rendle and his extensive experience with congregational systems. This does not mean that the purpose of the church is to make people unhappy! But I think it is essential to recognize the "happiness trap," as Rendle names it.[6] Can we just acknowledge: it is never possible to make everyone happy! When we think that our purpose is to make everyone completely happy about all things that happen in a congregation, we end up hamstringing the church's ability to make progress on a mission. Trying to make everyone happy turns our attention inward rather than outward. It allows the needs of certain individuals to overtake the needs of the whole and, in essence, to hold the congregation hostage. And on the individual level, it impairs the ability of people to really learn and open themselves up to the transformational opportunities of conflict.

In his excellent book, *Quietly Courageous*, Rendle explores this idea:

> One of the realities . . . is that in times of great turmoil, leaders are always asked to produce change—to make things different in their systems so that others will find a better future. But if asked for change, leaders will not be rewarded for the change produced, only for how well they keep things the same—following the known ways and the established rules so that they don't make people uncomfortable. It is the difference between management and leadership, following the old adage that management asks the question of whether we are doing things right, while leadership asks the question of whether we are doing right things.[7]

Without giving people the skills of working through these inevitable conflicts productively, congregational leadership that asks the important question of whether we are *doing right things* would quickly hit a wall of resistance.

IS TRANSFORMATION A CHOICE?

In the last decade or more, many of us in church leadership have had to confront the reality that churches and denominations must make dramatic changes in order to ably serve people as they live now. To help make those changes requires leadership in the way Rendle describes it, the kind of leadership that requires the ability to work *with* conflict, not try to resolve it. The skills of conflict transformation are not just helpful "add-on" skills, but, in fact, a necessary capacity to respond to the changing nature of religious community.

Sometimes the changes required emerge from a crisis within the community. The most dramatic example of this kind of crisis often comes about when a minister abuses his or her authority and engages in misconduct. I will be dedicating an entire chapter to this subject. But for now, I wish to note that while a great deal of pain and anguish can result from this experience, when leadership confronts the violation head on and with prayerful deliberation, clear boundaries, and honest engagement, the congregation can emerge stronger and healthier than ever before; in other words, transformed.

However, many of the challenges often come from outside the congregation. Today, in the age of trying to learn to do church in pandemic times, we can no longer ignore the need for developing the skills to make deep change. There will be some who will try to recreate the "old normal." But most of us realize that there is a new normal to be built, one that will require all of our courage and fortitude and willingness to meet conflict head on. A colleague recently put it this way: The pandemic gives us an opportunity (yes, opportunity!) to really explore what it means to grapple with complexity. How can we keep ourselves and one another safe? How can our congregations continue to thrive without the sustenance of in-person worship? These are not simple questions with simple answers.

Susan Beaumont addresses this kind of change in her book, *How to Lead When You Don't Know Where You Are Going.* She recognizes that doing ministry in these times is necessarily "liminal" work: "A liminal organization needs to unlearn old behaviors, challenge the status quo, experiment, take risks, and learn."[8] As explored in the work of William Bridges, Richard Rohr, and many others, liminal times require us to recognize that something has ended, something has been lost (even within the changes we have freely chosen and welcome). Changes don't simply go from ending to beginning. Engaging in a transition, rather than simply noting a change, requires us to go through a period of discomfort and disequilibrium, even of deep grief. As Bridges says,

> In other words, change is situational. Transition, on the other hand, is psychological. It is not those events, but rather the inner reorientation and self-redefinition that you have to go through in order to incorporate any of those changes into your life. Without a transition, a change is just a rearrangement of the furniture. Unless transition happens, the change won't work, because it doesn't "take."[9]

While this liminal time can be painful and fear-filled, it is also the place where transformation can happen. Richard Rohr defines it this way:

> It is the realm where God can best get at us because our false certitudes are finally out of the way. This is the sacred space where the old world is able to fall apart, and a bigger world is revealed. If we don't encounter liminal space in our lives, we start idealizing normalcy. The threshold is

God's waiting room. Here we are taught openness and patience as we come to expect an appointment with the divine Doctor.[10]

The pandemic is not the only crisis that requires us to go far deeper than change, into the realm of transformation. As a society we are being called to confront many assumptions about race and culture, White supremacy and hegemony. Those very words are enough to make our guts clench or just set many people's teeth on edge, even liberal White people. And yet the intransigence of the problems of violence and oppression toward people of color and other marginalized groups is clearly not something that can just be "solved." As the activist and organizer adrienne maree brown says,

> We won't end the systemic patterns of harm by isolating and picking off individuals, just as we can't limit the communicative power of mycelium by plucking a single mushroom from the dirt. We need to flood the entire system with life-affirming principles and practices, to clear the channels between us of the toxicity of supremacy, to heal from the harms of a legacy of devaluing some lives and needs in order to indulge others.[11]

To engage in this kind of transformation, she notes, will require us to become "excellent at being in conflict, which is a healthy, natural part of being human and biodiverse."[12]

The potential for conflict in congregations when we engage with this level of crisis and need for change is exponentially higher. Religious communities have often tried to ignore these cultural mudslides, hoping for a kind of willful "neutrality." Yet many are now learning that they do so at their peril, as they can all too easily get swept up in the chaos with no clear way to process what is happening.

A colleague described to me the crisis that unfolded when he and other lay leaders called for a "Black Lives Matter" banner to be hung outside their church to express solidarity with that movement. This prompted deeply held objections on the part of some, and many fraught and difficult discussions (discussions probably being too mild a word!). One woman in particular was terribly agitated and was the most outspoken critic in the meetings. My colleague finally spent some one-on-one time with her and engaged in a deeper conversation about what was at the heart of her concern. It emerged that she was terrified that violence would be visited upon the church. She had in mind the horrifying experiences of churches and synagogues in which a gunman has entered and killed those peacefully assembled in worship and prayer—a reality that is all too possible in our fractured and rageful world.

Instead of trying to talk her out of her fears, my colleague started to work *with* the concern. "How can we make the church a safer place?" he asked. She began to do some research on how churches have taken on this challenge and threw herself into helping create systems and practices that could help protect against potential violence, enlisting others who had similar concerns. Within a few weeks, she had changed from being adamantly against the banner, to one of its greatest advocates. Rather than sinking into fear and despair, she found a place of empowerment and strength. Transformation.

This is not work for the faint of heart. It requires learning skills that will not come naturally to us at first. It requires us to find practices that help quell our panic and hold us in a deeper place of learning. The challenges that lay before us will either wreak havoc in our religious communities, or they will help strengthen our courage and our resolve to find a new way of being in the world. What else is religious community for, other than to help nurture the ability for us as individuals and collectively as congregations to meet the cultural challenges that threaten to undermine the very fabric of human society?

In order to develop the skills to do this work, we must first look at and understand the complex physiological reactions that underlie our experiences of conflict. This is what we will explore in the next chapter.

Questions for Discussion

- What has been your personal pattern of responding to conflict?
- Have you experienced a conflict that went particularly bad? Can you say why?
- Have you experienced a conflict that seemed to turn out well? How so?
- Has your congregation engaged in these larger cultural conversations? How have these gone?

Chapter Two

The Physiology of Conflict

The body, not the thinking brain, is where we experience most of our pain, pleasure, and joy, and where we process most of what happens to us. It is also where we do most of our healing, including our emotional and psychological healing. And it is where we experience resilience and a sense of flow.

—Resmaa Menakem[1]

A ministerial intern I supervised once said this to me: "Whenever I see a conflict coming, I literally feel sick to my stomach and I start to pant! But when I see a conflict coming toward you, it almost looks like you relax into it and go still! How can I learn to do that and help reduce my anxiety?" My reply: "You've just taken the first and most important step: you recognize how it makes you feel."

This chapter will address more of the technical and biological aspects of what happens to our minds and bodies when we encounter conflict. I will turn to the personal and relational implications of this in subsequent chapters, but I think it is important to understand the "why" of what makes us react to conflict in order to find ways to open ourselves up to the possibility of transformation.

In this hyper-polarized world, we have had to confront the reality that conflicts are not just about "facts" that we can clarify. They are not even about the words we use. Words like "liberty," "oppression," "freedom," and "justice" can mean entirely different things to different people. Ashli Babbitt, the woman who was unfortunately killed during

19

the attack on the U.S. Capitol on January 6, 2021, had a sign hanging on her door: "Tyranny, lawlessness, disrespect and hatred for our fellow man will not be tolerated." Probably any of us would agree with this sentiment. And yet she interpreted it to mean that she should join others in a violent assault on innocent people. Some of us experience this great chasm of political difference within our families or in our religious communities, and feel this difference of perception and definition all too viscerally. Are we really even speaking the same language?

Even when we find ourselves disagreeing with someone with whom we usually agree, it challenges us in ways that go beyond just a mind-muddle. If all conflicts were a matter of simply coming to agreement about established facts, we would not have that much difficulty with them. The way the phrase "false facts" has entered our national dialogue is evidence of this. It is rarely that simple, and yet we often try to "reason" our way out of them. But much of our response to conflict happens in parts of our bodies and our brains that we may rarely be fully cognizant of, rather than a result of "rationality." Why is this the case? Where does this cognitive dissonance come from? Some of the answers to these conundrums can be found in our bodies and our brains. Or, as noted by Resmaa Menakem, "The body, not the thinking brain, is where we experience most of our pain, pleasure, and joy, and where we process most of what happens to us."[2]

THE LIZARD BRAIN

Let's begin by taking a look at the amygdala, or the brain stem, that part of the brain that's usually known as the "lizard brain." It is called this because part of the brain of every living being (including lizards!) functions in the same way. Research about the amygdala shows that it is important to our ability to process and store information about a variety of emotions, but its most commonly understood function is how it responds to fear.

Those wishing to understand neuroscience in much greater detail would benefit from Louis Cozolino's book, *The Neuroscience of Psychotherapy*.[3] I find Cozolino's descriptions of the workings of the amygdala particularly enlightening. Essentially what he describes is that we have two systems that help us process fear and danger: one is incredibly fast, the other much slower and methodical. The amygdala is responsible for the fast response, as in *lightning fast*. Imagine you are walking down a path and suddenly encounter a snake. Before your conscious brain has a chance to really formulate a thought like "SNAKE: RUN!" the amygdala has already sent a message to your vagal nervous system to immediately require a response. It can change how you breathe in a nanosecond. Depending on the situation, the message may be: "Breathe faster!" so that you can prepare yourself to run (or fight, if you're so inclined). Or it may be: "Breathe slower!" so that you can prepare to freeze. It can slow your digestive system so that all of your energy goes to dealing with the crisis (think of how our gut clenches) as well as many other autonomic responses.

Cozolino describes this response as the "amygdala hijack."[4] The amygdala thinks in very binary terms: danger/not danger. It doesn't want to spend a lot of time analyzing what kind of snake it might be or what pretty coloring it may have. Therefore, it can actually impede the functioning of the neocortex, which engages in all kinds of analyses and complex cogitations. The amygdala response is so quick, you are rarely conscious of it until you reflect upon it later. It is quick, but not necessarily accurate; it falls back on stereotypes you may have internalized without being conscious of them. It creates a kind of imaginative gridlock that requires us to *react*, rather than to *respond*.

As I have noted, this happens completely below the level of consciousness, even when we feel threatened by something different than physical dangers. The amygdala can be triggered when we feel that someone is angry at us, when someone we trusted betrays us, or when it becomes clear that what we value most isn't valued by others. If someone has buried trauma, it can be activated by experiences that create a reaction that may seem incomprehensible to others, even to the person suffering the trauma.

So, to put it more simply: people who are in what I sometimes jokingly call a "highly amygdalated state" simply can't think straight. It is almost impossible to "reason" with someone who doesn't have easy access to their reason. One could argue that the deep conflicts in our culture have traumatized all of us and leave us at the mercy of our amygdalas, which makes factual conversation seem almost futile.

ATTACHMENT SYSTEMS

Not only does the amygdala respond in the moment; it also encodes memories of fearful experiences so that we can learn to avoid them in the future. In particular, our childhood experiences of trauma become encoded in ways that influence the rest of our lives. The amygdala is one of the major players in what is called the "attachment system." We most often think about attachment when we contemplate attachment "disorders," but the reality is that each of us has an attachment system that guides our responses to challenges in both helpful and unhelpful ways. In *Attachment in Adulthood*, Mario Mikulincer and Philip Shaver helpfully explore the ways in which the attachment systems that we developed in childhood follow us into our adult lives and our behaviors and perceptions.[5]

Essentially, Mikulincer and Shaver outline three main categories of attachment systems: secure attachment, anxious attachment, and avoidant attachment. If a person grows up in an environment in which they receive support and protection from their parents when they feel threatened, they can ideally develop patterns in which they can feel secure even in the face of many fearful occurrences, and do not become hamstrung by imagining fearful consequences in the future. They have a lifelong pattern of knowing how to soothe their amygdala and can thereby engage the world with more curiosity and creativity. By contrast, those who experience inconsistent protection and affection can develop a system of anxious attachment, in which they constantly seek reassurances about their safety and connection. Their amygdalas are on constant alert. For those who had very little expectation of comfort in their childhood, a pattern of avoidance develops in which it is difficult to allow themselves to be vulnerable or trust others. By avoiding connection, they avoid triggering their amygdala with its painful collection of memories of neglect.

Certainly, none of us is a perfect example of one of the three types named above, but these categories do help us understand how the amygdala is conditioned to respond in particular ways. In the next chapter I'll talk about strategies for coming to terms with our attachment systems, but for now I want to note that religious communities are, in effect, tinder boxes for our attachment systems to erupt. Often people come to a congregation to find the kind of protection and affection that may have been lacking in their childhood, and therefore can react in often inexplicable ways when that connection may be threatened. In addition, people can often transfer their experiences with their parents as "attachment figures" to their religious leaders.[6] All of us who are clergy have inevitably had experiences with lay people who project their parental issues on us. Often it is hard to recognize when that is happening in the moment, and it is quite uncomfortable to feel like we are the cause of deep pain in our people, even when we know logically that it is not our fault.

Beyond the experiences of childhood, our experience of trauma of other kinds can manifest in ways that often seem irrational. There is considerable new research about the impact of trauma on our nervous system. Remember, the amygdala is also a part of the brain that creates vivid memories, both positive and negative. If we experience something that reminds us of a past traumatic experience, even something as innocuous as an odor, the amygdala can get stimulated all over again, once again making it difficult to have access to our "reasoning" brain. Anyone who has worked with those suffering from post-traumatic stress disorder (PTSD) will recognize the futility of trying to "explain" how irrational their responses are.

INTERGENERATIONAL TRAUMA

The trauma that we experience may not just have impact on ourselves, but even on our descendants. According to new research, "your experiences during your lifetime—particularly traumatic ones—would have a very real impact on your family for generations to come. There are a growing number of studies that support the idea that the effects of trauma can reverberate down the generations through epigenetics."[7]

For example, studies of men who were held in prisoner-of-war camps during the Civil War—where they experienced horrific treatment and deprivations—show that the soldiers' *subsequent generations* suffered higher-than-average mortality rates, even when taking into account other genetic factors. This seems to happen not through altering genetic DNA code, but by attaching RNA code that can trigger a cortisol reaction to a particular stimulus, even when that person did not experience the original trauma. Researchers have shown that by creating a traumatic experience in mice while they encounter something as innocuous as the scent of cherry blossoms, their progeny will also react to that scent with panic.

RACIALIZED TRAUMA

When we apply this research to some of our most entrenched societal problems, most especially racism, it can be both illuminating and deeply disturbing. Resmaa Menakem is a psychiatrist, healer, and compelling speaker and writer on the effects of racialized trauma. In his excellent book, *My Grandmother's Hands*, he introduces the concept:

> When European settlers first came to this country centuries ago, they brought a millennium of intergenerational and historical trauma with them, stored in the cells of their bodies. Today, this trauma continues to live on in the bodies of most Americans. Most white immigrants to the New World didn't heal from their trauma. Instead, beginning a little over three centuries ago, they created the concepts of whiteness, of blackness (and redness and yellowness), and of white-body supremacy. Then they blew much of their trauma through the bodies of Africans and their descendants. This served to embed trauma in Black bodies, but it did nothing to mend the trauma in white ones. Much of our current culture—and most of our current cultural divides—are built around this trauma.[8]

Menakem says that the way those of us who are White-identified have responded to this trauma, whether recognized or not, is to strategize or think our way out of it.[9] A trauma that is experienced by the body has to counter it with another kind of bodily experience, not just reasonable thought. Rather than just *explaining* racism, Menakem's book introduces embodied practices that can help hold us through the difficult process of acknowledging the truth of these painful legacies and work through them.

These embodied practices—including meditation, visualization, and rhythm creation—are helpful practices for soothing reactivity, no matter the stimulus. Interestingly, the same nerve system that the amygdala relies upon, the vagal nervous system, can also be employed to help calm us down. Simply by consciously changing our breathing, we can reverse the reactivity.

Singer/songwriter Darden Smith created an incredibly powerful program for soldiers who suffer from PTSD to process their experiences and to help them heal. He and other songwriters take participants on a retreat in which they deeply listen to the soldier's stories, and then co-create a song out of the experience.

The hope is that the songwriting will provide a healthy emotional outlet for the service members, and the resulting songs will be a source of pride, a help to others facing similar challenges, and a bridge in the gap between military service and civilian life.[10] As Smith describes:

> We all have a story. . . . When we listen, and listen well enough to take the soldiers' words and turn them into art, and sing it back to them, something happens. What it is, I don't know. I'm a songwriter, not a therapist. But something happens, and it's powerful.[11]

And, indeed, it works:

> Chirco still tears up when he listens to his song "I'm Not Supposed to Be Here," which touches on everything from his accidental conception to his survivor's guilt. "The songwriters take the worst thing that has ever happened to you and turn it into something beautiful," he says. "The experience energized me and really set me back on the path to healing."[12]

Trauma works through and within the body. And the body, with all its senses and subliminal emotional processes, is the most important partner in our healing.

I'll go into more detail in the next chapter about strategies for lowering reactivity in ourselves, but here I want to focus on the most successful strategy when we encounter reactivity in others: reminding them that they are loved and cared for. This is the function of the mammalian parts of our brain.

THE BENEFIT OF CONNECTION

Instead of arguing with and confronting a reactive person, it is often far more helpful to reassure them that your relationship is important. Remember that our attachment systems have developed in response to feeling either connected or disconnected. The amygdala is calling out to be soothed. It often feels difficult to respond in this way when someone is berating us or accusing us or misrepresenting what we have said or done. By reaching out, it can feel like we are capitulating or agreeing with them. But, as I'll talk about in a subsequent chapter, *listening does not have to imply agreement.*

Utilizing this connecting response is particularly important in the context of congregational life. Isn't helping people feel loved, cared for, and important one of the greatest purposes of religious community? Conversely, if someone feels like that connection and love have been inhibited because of a conflict, their reactivity could increase in intensity. In this sense, congregations hold one of the most important keys for unlocking conflict, just as conflict in congregations takes on a different level of magnitude because of the importance of the relationships.

Back to the exploration of how the brain works: creating connection is essentially stimulating the more complex parts of the mammalian brain that emphasize the pleasure of social contact, thus allowing us to slow down and be less reactive. Mammals look to community for survival, and therefore from our earliest days we learn to pay attention to social cues and social constraints. Again, congregational life helps reinforce both of these, sometimes to our benefit and sometimes to our detriment.

We learn that we must behave in certain ways to help us stay in the good graces of the tribe, which helps us feel safer and more relaxed. But we also learn that behaviors that go against the grain of our culture can result in our expulsion. Therefore, if our culture is one that tells us it is not okay to be angry or to engage in conflict (which many Eurocentric cultures do), then we may end up stifling what could be a productive engagement with conflict. This is not to say that we shouldn't offer reassurances of connection, as I mentioned above. But be attentive to how some reassurances may only serve to bury conflict rather than engage with it.

Much of the processing that takes place in the mammalian parts of the brain can also be subconscious. We may not be aware that we are changing our behaviors to *fit in*, as we integrate this knowledge over the course of time and experience (sometimes hard-earned). Therefore, if we wish to help people overcome their aversion to conflict, we may have to redouble (or triple, or quadruple!) our efforts to affirm connection without tying that connection to agreement.

INTEGRATING THE RIGHT AND LEFT BRAIN

To take us further down the rabbit hole of brain science, I want to refer to some recent work by the neurobiologist Iain McGilchrist, who has made us think differently about why the brain is divided into two hemispheres.[13] He's not just doing a superficial study of why we have a left brain and a right brain, something we have heard from pseudo-scientists before. In fact, those pseudo-scientists ended up poisoning the well of the study of why our brain is divided so much that serious scientists wouldn't touch it. Much to our detriment, as it turns out.

McGilchrist has discovered that there are indeed profound differences between the two hemispheres of the brain. They are different sizes, different shapes and weights, and have different cellular architecture, just to name a few. Every living being has a divided brain because we're trying to solve a basic dilemma in life: we need to do different things *simultaneously*, things that are completely different from each other.

Birds and animals—for they, too, all have divided brains—have to solve a conundrum every moment of their waking lives. In order to make use of the world, to manipulate it to their own ends, they need to pay narrowly focused attention to what they have already prioritized as of significance to them. A bird needs to be able, for example, to pick out a seed against the background of grit on which it lies, to pick up a particular twig to build a nest, and so on.

But if that is the only attention it is paying, it will soon end up as someone else's lunch while it is getting its own because it needs at the same time to pay a quite different type of attention to the world—a broad, open, sustained vigilance, without any preconception of what it is that may be found, be it predator or mate, foe or friend. How to pay such contrary types of attention to the world at once? It is like patting your head and rubbing your stomach at the same time—but worse, because one consciousness can't be committed to two kinds of attention simultaneously.[14]

This is where the bicameral mind comes in. The different hemispheres allow us to do both things simultaneously: to pay narrow beam attention which enables us to get and grasp, as well as to keep an open mind to what can be, connections that can be made or explored or related to. In other words, it is the left brain's job to narrow things down to a certainty and the right brain's job to open up to possibility. We are doing this all the time. Each part of the brain is doing its own thing and then leaving it up to that little section in between to make the choices about which we attend to. Kind of staggers the imagination, doesn't it?

But McGilchrist also asserts that our western culture has been dogmatically giving the left brain the largest say, and denigrating—or at least not attending to—the meaning-making work of the right brain. By constantly asking for the facts and the proof of the matter, we end up cutting ourselves off from a larger and more meaningful truth. In fact, scientists have studied what happens when you only allow one part of the brain to function. When only the left brain functions, it literally cannot tell right from wrong. There is no morality to a brain that is only interested in manipulating the universe. A scary thought indeed, that this is what our culture values the most.

As I noted above, simply delivering facts to someone does not impact how they feel about what we are doing or saying. The left brain gives us those all-important facts, but the right brain helps us to *make meaning* of them, to contextualize them, to understand what came before, what's happening now, and what could happen in the future. In essence, the right brain is the storytelling part of the brain, and it explains why telling *a story* about what is happening is far more helpful in a conflictual situation than simply relating the facts.

Again, relating this to congregational life can be illuminating. Certainly, through our religious practices and texts we are helping people make meaning of the confusing and distressing world around them: we are telling them stories to help them make sense of it. So, let's apply this to congregational conflicts: helping people tell the stories of why they are reacting the way that they are, rather than demanding facts about why they are reacting, is far more useful and effective.

Understanding the ways in which the right brain and left brain work together also helps us grasp the way we quickly make assumptions about things and then believe that our assumptions are the same as reality!

THE LADDER OF INFERENCE

To help explain how we make assumptions, I will turn to a tool, the "ladder of inference"[15] (figure 2.1). As we've already noted, it is the left brain's job to take in information and data, while the right brain helps us interpret that data. But it becomes all too easy to believe that our interpretation *is* the data.

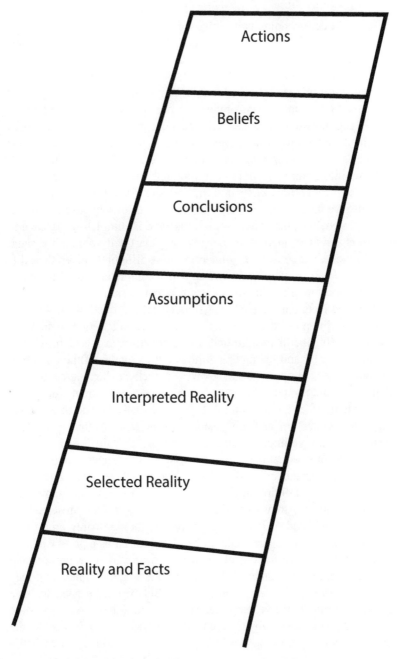

Figure 2.1. The ladder of inference. *Developed by Chris Argyris.*

It would be physiologically impossible for the brain to observe and note every single bit of reality around us. There simply isn't room in our brains to hold all that information! So, even before we begin to observe, we employ the right brain to help us choose *what* to observe. Already there is interpretation involved in this. Why is this fact more important than another? It may seem obvious to me why I choose to attend to something, but someone else could make a completely different choice of what to attend to for a completely understandable reason. But their choice is *already different* than mine. As we take in more and more data, we make more and more interpretations and selections and quickly *make our way up the ladder* into the realm of assumptions and beliefs. Because we have been climbing our own ladder in subconscious ways, we tend to believe that where we have arrived is completely logical and apparent. And yet, again, someone else may start with some of the same observations, but because they interpret these differently given their different experiences, they could end up with a completely different belief, and are therefore climbing up a very different ladder.

Ann and Kenneth were college students whose relationship had developed to the point that they decided to move in together. Ann came from a fairly liberal background, but Kenneth was raised in a strict Catholic family, and his mother followed the dictates of the church to the letter: the idea of premarital sex was anathema to her. Kenneth knew that she would not take the news of their new arrangement well, so he put off telling her his plans until they had actually moved in together! He finally called her and fairly soon into the conversation Ann could hear his mother yelling: "What about the baby?!" Baby, what baby?

After his mother calmed down a bit, Kenneth managed to get her to "walk down the ladder" and together they deciphered this: Fact: Ann and Kenneth were living in the same house and sharing the same bed. Selected reality: if they were sharing the same bed, they must be having sex. Interpreted reality: if they have sex, they probably aren't taking any precautions since Kenneth had been raised as a good Catholic and wouldn't use birth control. Assumption: if they have unprotected sex, she would get pregnant. Conclusion: if Ann got pregnant and they weren't married, the baby would suffer. Belief: babies need to have married parents to thrive. Ergo action: how could they have done such a thing to an innocent baby? In Kenneth's mother's mind, it was like the baby was already a living, breathing thing! What about the baby?! We climb such ladders all the time without realizing that we have created babies when in fact there are none.

When someone questions our conclusions and beliefs, let alone our actions, it can be mystifying and often disturbing that they don't see the world in the same way that we do. If we are both teetering at the top of our ladders, only throwing our conclusions at each other, we will end up with what may feel like an irreconcilable conflict. The babies that exist only in our minds can still feel like living, breathing beings under threat.

Jerome was a young, ambitious, and charismatic minister who had recently been called to an urban church that had a storied history of dynamic engagement in the city's social justice issues. In recent years, however, that involvement had slowed. It felt to Jerome as if the church was still trading on its past reputation, and utilizing outdated strategies, without really engaging in an impactful way. An opportunity arose in the immediate community to become involved in a community-based interfaith organizing project. Jerome was excited by the possibilities this presented and started to move, full steam ahead, to get the congregation to agree.

At a subsequent board meeting Jerome was startled to find that the board president did not support the project and in fact adamantly opposed it. Jerome felt blindsided by this and started to nurse feelings of betrayal. He assumed that the opposition was due to the president's desire to avoid controversial methods, and started organizing support to thwart her opposition. What had begun as a productive partnership between Jerome and the board president quickly deteriorated into a polarized standoff. The president began to collect stories about how Jerome wasn't fulfilling his pastoral duties, which diminished the board's support of him. He continued to push the issue in a congregational meeting at which the president revealed that her opposition actually had to do with a painful experience of humiliation she had with one of the projects' chief organizers. The proposal failed when the president shared this difficult story. Jerome had never really tried to understand what was at the heart of her concerns, and the whole project dissolved into feelings of hurt and frustration.

Often, we get to this stalemated place, completely mystified about what has happened. It is so easy to assume that everyone sees the world the same way we do. And our way of seeing things is obvious, right? Without checking our assumptions at key moments along the way, a major disruption in what had been a previously trusting relationship can occur.

Later in the book I will talk about ways we can help *walk people back down their ladders* to get at what might be a more shared reality. But let's stay for a moment with the realization that the conflict didn't occur because of the facts. It occurred because of the *assumptions and conclusions drawn*, and the assumptions and conclusions we draw are *unique to us*. In very homogenous communities it may be that people are walking up very similar ladders, but even the slightest variation can take people in very different directions.

The more I understand about the ways our bodies and minds operate at a level beneath our consciousness, the more I can feel overwhelmed with a sense of hopelessness. Are we really not fully in control of ourselves? Are our assumptions really that different from others? Unfortunately, the evidence says yes. But it is also true that there are some aspects of ourselves that *are* within our control. And it is possible to come to some semblance of agreement. In the next chapter I will talk about ways to develop a greater degree of self-awareness and thereby, self-control, as well as how we can learn to test our assumptions in a productive way.

If I can remind myself that people exist on ladders that are different from one another, I can begin to develop a greater degree of compassion for others. It is so easy to interpret people's behaviors as intentionally oppositional, when in fact there is an encyclopedia of embedded stories in each person, stories of which I, and perhaps that individual, are completely unaware.

And shouldn't we, as religious communities, understand that we always work at the intersection of mystery and the mundane? That giving people an opportunity to connect their stories to something larger than themselves is perhaps the greatest gift we can offer? Remembering this purpose can help strengthen us to face the pain of conflict in order to get to the place of telling a new story.

Questions for Discussion

- Think of a time when you were going through a very difficult conflict. How did it feel in your body? Where did you feel it in your body? Does just thinking about it make you *feel* it again?

- Do you remember a time when someone you were in conflict with seemed to have an entirely different understanding of reality than you? Can you describe the differences? Can you identify the different assumptions at work?
- Have you seen examples of conflicts in your congregation, when people seemed to be talking past each other?

Chapter Three

Revelations of the Self

True belonging is the spiritual practice of believing in and belonging to yourself so deeply that you can share your most authentic self
with the world and find sacredness in both being a part of something
and standing alone in the wilderness. True belonging doesn't require
you to change who you are; it requires you to be who you are.

—Brené Brown[1]

As the previous chapter helps us to see, there is much about ourselves
that we cannot consciously know, and sometimes cannot consciously
control. It can be daunting to face all the ways in which we might be
mysteries to ourselves, as well as to others. But there are important
and helpful strategies for combing through the strands of feelings and
beliefs and behaviors to find some coherent path to self-understanding,
and thus useful strategies for healthy interactions with others.

A WORD TO CLERGY

Let me begin by addressing myself to my clergy colleagues. Leadership in congregations today requires deliberately honing our ability to
engage in deep self-awareness and to find the practices that best help
us to moderate our anxiety and reactivity. Clergy certainly ought to
know this, as we are by far the most powerful players in congregational
systems. And yet I'm often surprised to find when I conduct workshops

for clergy that not all—and sometimes only a few—can identify their best practices. So let me be clear: I believe the most important skill in ministry is to set aside your own needs and wants in service of a larger mission. But, as my spiritual director once said to me, in order to let go of your ego, you need to first *understand* your ego.

If we look again at the work I described earlier about attachment systems, it would be easy to feel like we are stuck in our own attachment story without an ability to change it. While it is certainly true that our most formative experiences as children have profound impacts on us, there is always an opportunity to begin to tell a new story. After all, the possibility for redemption is a core principle in any religious tradition. I speak not necessarily of redemption from sin, but redemption from pain.

The three patterns of attachment systems—secure, anxious, and avoidant—can help us understand the consequences of certain kinds of childhood experiences in our adult lives. But these categories are not completely discreet. I don't know anyone who had a completely secure childhood with just the right amount of love and comfort offered when needed! Any of us can become anxious about our relationships under certain circumstances, leading us to seek reassurance. I imagine all of us have avoided difficult feelings at times and can be uncomfortable with vulnerability. The question is not what category we fall in, but what our current behaviors tell us about possibly unresolved wounds from the past.

We need not plumb every painful experience of our past to move forward into our future, but it does behoove us to become aware of the kinds of experiences that have become our triggers. These triggers make it difficult to remain present to whatever is happening around us, and can contribute to the feeling of being lost in the reactivity of our amygdalated memory. A colleague recently said to me: "After 30-plus years in the ministry I am finally learning that when I act out of a reactive place, it always turns out badly! Now if I can just learn to recognize when I am being reactive, I'll be okay!" We've all written that fiery email that will explain perfectly why we are right. We've all snapped at someone who simply wasn't aware that they were acting like our judgmental brother. We've all delivered that prophetic sermon that surely made it clear how misjudged we have been. None of us is perfect, and we are all capable of behaving badly. The question is: *What have we learned about ourselves from our mistakes?*

Engaging in self-reflection through journaling, prayer, meditation, or any other spiritual practice is essential. And it may not be sufficient. I believe that we all need partners in our self-discernment, people who can mirror back to us that which we may be unable or unwilling to see. Whether it be a therapist, spiritual director, colleague, friend, or spouse, finding a trusted person who can listen us back into a new way of being can do more for our ministry than any seminary course ever can.

In my own case, I have had a multitude of therapists who have each helped me see something that I really didn't want to surface, and yet once revealed, I was able to set it aside and move on. I benefited greatly from seven years of spiritual direction in which I could work through my attachment-figure issues (which we all have) and thereby come into a life-giving awareness of how God works in my life. And I still have work to do.

I often say that the great thing about being an interim minister is that we learn that it is not about us! Since our ministries are short (as some would say—we are pre-fired), it is much easier to see that the frustrations that people may have with us are often really about a ministry in the past. The work is primarily about giving the ministry back to the people.

But the hardest part of being an interim minister is to come face to face with those legacies of previous ministries that have done great harm to congregations. I have seen the ways in which anxious ministers have put their own needs before that of their people, thereby making themselves the focus of the ministry, rather than the mission of the congregation. I have felt the pain of rejection and confusion from lay people whose minister offered more judgment and diffidence than love. And, let me also be clear, I have been inspired to witness the fruits of transformational ministry that led to growth and vitality.

Sometimes all three of these results have come *from the same minister.* None of us is perfect. All of us are works in progress. The question is, how much do we devote ourselves to our learning and development? We can bemoan all we like about being giant projection screens for our people. *And it will ever be thus.* How we assume the mantle of responsibility that comes with those projections will be the defining nature of our ministry.[2] As Brené Brown reminds us, "True belonging doesn't

require you to change who you are; it requires you to be who you are."[3]
This does not mean that our selves are immutable, as we are always
learning and changing on the surface, but that we must come to terms
with the core of who we are and recognize when these core concerns
need to be met.

Elizabeth is a minister who has enjoyed considerable success. The
congregation she served for 16 years grew in numbers and in engagement with the larger community. She is a skilled fundraiser and raised
several million dollars during an economic turndown that allowed the
church to build a much-needed addition for the growing religious education program. She was less skilled in managing staff, however. She
had a hard time establishing her authority with the staff, as she was very
keen on being seen as likable and often avoided conflict. An associate minister who was called about halfway during Elizabeth's tenure
grew very frustrated with this lack of leadership. She began to actively
undermine her with the board and built an unhealthy alliance with the
administrator. Elizabeth saw some of this happening and bemoaned the
state of affairs with her colleagues, but failed to confront the associate.
She took a four-month sabbatical and when she returned, the board
was already primed to reduce her management authority. Elizabeth had
completely overestimated her support on the board and could not regain
her footing. She was forced to resign soon after. If Elizabeth had been
more aware earlier in her tenure of the level of frustration with her lack
of definitive leadership, she could have done the hard work of examining the roots of her conflict avoidance. Her ministry, which had been
very effective in many ways, could have been saved.

None of this means that we must be all things to all people. Again,
none of us are perfect. We need not become doormats to our congregations' endless demands. What it does mean is that it is our first
obligation in the midst of any challenge to discern our own part in the
drama—even if it is only a bit part. It also means that we are obligated
to set and uphold appropriate boundaries.

Christine served a church during a time when she needed a lot of
personal support. She and her husband had two young children, and
their life was often chaotic. She joined a parenting group that also
included a couple who were members of her church. They recognized
immediately that they had much in common, and started having dinner
at one another's homes and getting their kids together for play dates.

After a few months of this, however, Christine began to recognize the ways in which this friendship was starting to erode other relationships in the church. People assumed she had a "favorite" and felt jealous of the relationship. The other couple also enjoyed gossiping about other members of the church, which impacted Christine's view of them. She started to impose more boundaries on the relationship, and the other couple became furious. They began to undermine her ministry and caused considerable damage that took several years to work through.

Ministry is incredibly lonely work. Given how much time we spend with our congregations, it can be hard to find the time and energy to try to find and engage in friendships elsewhere. When we feel like a congregant really understands and supports us, it is all too easy to fall into a relationship that may have dangerous consequences. It is impossible to treat every member of the congregation equally, and we all inevitably blur the lines with parishioners. But we do so at our peril, as well as the peril of the congregant and the congregation. Developing awareness of these lines, even when we sometimes cross over them, is imperative.

We must recognize that the pandemic has created even more demands on ministry beyond our already burdened list of duties. The pastor and writer, Jenny Smith, wrote a blog post that beautifully describes this state of exhausted functioning:

We just ran a marathon.
We closed our doors to in-person worship.
We figured out online worship. Maybe. Kind of.
We received email after email from frustrated congregants.
We felt the brunt of unprocessed grief in our communities.
We tried to continue as many ministries as we could sustain.
We dreamed up new ones.
We crashed and burned.
We wondered if giving would continue.
We became video chat professionals.
We spent hours looking at black screens summoning sermons to write themselves.
We ached with isolation.
We spoke hope and grace and possibility.
We questioned our call to ministry.
We agonized over the safest ways to return to in-person gatherings.
We took a few days off here and there, trying to find solid ground to rest on.

We smiled on camera as if we could stir our hearts to life with our own pleading.

We received grace and stunning kindness from people in our communities.

We watched colleagues look like they had it together. But we guessed they didn't either.

Then we opened our doors to in-person worship again.

We crossed the finish line! We made it! We did a hard thing!

Then . . .

Instead of collapsing at the finish lie in a heap.

Instead of drinking water.

Instead of resting our aching bodies.

Something else happened.

An official-looking race organizer slapped another number on our back and pushed us toward another starting line that mysteriously appeared.

Wait. What?

A second marathon? Right now?[4]

Ministry is incredibly hard in the best of circumstances. But right now the pressure is exponentially higher. As I will discuss later, this requires that we acknowledge we are not perfect, nor are we superheroes. I have shared this blog post with my lay leadership, and they have now adopted the language; "Are we trying to run when you need us to walk?" Sometimes just naming our limitations and realities is sufficient.

But again, in times like these, it behooves us even more to find practices that help sustain us. Jenny Smith offers one herself, called the "Your Palms Up Life," a bi-monthly reflection email that helps us bring our attention down to ourselves.[5] Every colleague I know finds this self-sustenance difficult right now. But without it, we risk injury to ourselves, as well as injury to others, when we don't recognize our own reactivity of the moment.

THE FIRST TASK OF CONFLICT TRANSFORMATION

And now to the work of all of us: the first task of conflict transformation is to resist the temptation to completely blame others and look at our own contribution to the situation.

First of all, let us recognize the physical signs of how we can be caught up in reactivity: our breathing may have changed, our gut may feel butterflies or alligators, our vision may have narrowed, our hackles may have risen. If we've learned anything from the previous chapter, it should be that *none of us ever behaves well or productively in this state.* Even if we are not doing active harm, we have cut ourselves off from being able to explore the situation creatively and thoughtfully. That amygdala has hijacked our system. And reactivity begets reactivity. Our amygdala is hyper-attentive to whenever anyone else seems to be on edge, and starts to activate in sympathy. So not only are we not helping ourselves, we are creating a reactive system.

The first order of business when this happens is to forget about business: *breathe.* The benefits of taking back control of your respiratory system cannot be overstated. That one simple act says to the amygdala: *stand down.* Take your time. Leave the room if you have to. Walk up and down the hall for a few minutes. Do whatever you can to prevent the mental lockdown that comes from letting your amygdala run the show.

For me, some of the most important insights from recent work on the impact of trauma has been the realization of what helps to ease it. As mentioned in the previous chapter, Resmaa Menakem's work in particular pairs intellectual awareness with embodied practices that help hold us in a place of processing pain. Each chapter in his book has accompanying suggested practices that are as important as the insights that he offers. He explains that

> our bodies have a form of knowledge that is different from our cognitive brains. This knowledge is typically experienced as a felt sense of constriction or expansion, pain or ease, energy or numbness. Often this knowledge is stored in our bodies as wordless stories about what is safe and what is dangerous.[6]

We may not think that sitting in a boardroom with other congregants could trigger those stories, but we ignore at our peril the fact that those stories have great power within us.

Simone was chairing an important fundraising effort that was fundamental to fulfilling the budget for the year. She became more and more brusque with committee members and started undervaluing their contributions or taking projects back to work on herself. The minister brought her in to talk about what was happening. She began by expressing her frustrations with everyone on the committee. But after a deeper conversation, she started to realize that she was remembering a project she had been responsible for a few years back, one that had ended in failure. The failure wasn't necessarily her fault, but she felt terribly guilty about it nonetheless and her current controlling behavior was a result of this sense of guilt. She could feel herself seizing up with tension just talking about it. The minister helped her see what had been happening in the larger system so that her sense of guilt eased. And he helped her develop some breathing exercises that she could use whenever she felt that sense of heightened responsibility coming down on her. Her leadership of the committee became more empowering, and the project came off with success. It wasn't perfect, but it was still effective, and Simone was able to laugh about some of the things that went wrong without again feeling like a failure.

Not all of us would understand ourselves as traumatized people, but everyone has experienced trauma of one kind or another that is still encoded in our minds and bodies. And the strategies that help traumatized people recover actually help all of us regain our sense of equilibrium. Interestingly, those strategies are often a part of what congregations practice, particularly in worship: breathing, finding a rhythm, humming, grounding our bodies in place—aren't these what we do? It makes me think that our liturgical practices, whether we are conscious of it or not, have developed as a response to trauma and offer ways of healing even to those who are not aware of their harm.

The poet David Whyte explores the sense of overwhelm that happens when we feel like the expectations placed on us may be too much to bear:

> Besieged is how most people feel most of the time: by events, by people, by all the necessities of providing, parenting or participating . . .
>
> To feel crowded, set upon, blocked by circumstances, in defeat or victory, is not only the daily experience of most human beings in most contemporary societies; it has been an abiding dynamic of individual life since the dawn of human consciousness. . . .
>
> If the world will not go away then the great discipline seems to be the ability to make an identity that can live in the midst of everything without feeling beset. Being besieged asks us to begin the day not with a to do list but a not to do list, a moment outside of the time bound world in which it

can be re-ordered and re-prioritized. In this space of undoing and silence we create a foundation from which to re-imagine our day and ourselves.[7]

It occurs to me that this is exactly what worship and spiritual practices can help us do: "to create a foundation from which to re-imagine our day and ourselves." When congregational life gives people the opportunity to deeply engage in these practices, we offer a strategy for letting go of reactivity.

Transformation requires creativity and openness and exploration. Reactivity is the opposite of this. Whatever strategies that you can employ to break the cycle of thoughtless reaction will help bring you to possibilities you may never have considered.

SYSTEMS THEORY

Understanding ourselves has many more dimensions than just measuring our own reactivity. As I said in the introduction, there is no such thing as a completely discreet self. Nevertheless, each self has inherent gifts and attributes that are important for us to sort through to get to a place of understanding what we need from, and what we can offer to, community. Those of you with experience in systems theory will recognize this as the work of self-differentiation, a key concept in family systems theory—a set of theories that has a long and important lineage, particularly as applied to congregational life.[8] Its concepts have been more formative to my ministry than almost any other philosophy. It helps us to recognize the difference between *process* and *content*. Focusing on content, i.e. "the facts of the matter," can completely miss the complexity of dynamics that often have little to do with the facts.

A particularly accessible exploration of what family systems theory has to teach congregation is *Anxious Church, Anxious People*, by Jack Shitama.

> A family systems view helps us to look at our interactions to understand what is going on in the system and with others. For example, in a church meeting, people can disagree in any number of ways. They can self-differentiate, using "I" statements in a non-anxious way. They can self-define, but not engage (narcissism). They can spew anxiety at everyone in sight. They can clam up and not take a stand at all, even if they disagree.

> Notice that I haven't named a topic or issue. That would be content, and content is irrelevant from a leadership standpoint. What's important is that the way people respond helps us to understand the processes at work in the system. And understanding these processes can help us to be more effective as a leader.[9]

Again, there are many aspects of family systems theory that are incredibly helpful for creating a space for learning about ourselves and others. But I often find it challenging to explain to lay people, and some of its core tenets can be problematic when taken to extremes.

Let us look again at the concept of non-anxious presence, which requires regulating our emotions as well as not allowing ourselves to get caught up in the emotions of others. Understanding and owning our own personal goals and values helps keep us from the trap of trying to make everyone happy. I am definitely in favor of this! However, the way self-differentiation is often taught seems to present a model of self in which we can step out of our emotions, much as we might step out of our sweaty gym clothes.

Practitioners such as Edwin Friedman were trying to correct for a culture that emphasized sameness and lack of conflict, which I completely understand and honor. It is just this wall that conflict transformation often comes up against. But by emphasizing the need for a *mastery* of emotions, it would be easy to see why this would be interpreted as emotions being *bad*. It is a model, in short, that shaves a bit too closely to concepts of White male superiority. In particular, feminist practitioners have pointed to a lack of awareness of the dynamics of power in relationships that is often present in the classic presentations of family systems theory. Some practitioners of color share the critique about needing to address imbalanced power, and also have brought a great deal of criticism to the idea of the complete autonomy of self, pointing out that in communities of color, interdependence and interrelationship is not just a preference, but often a matter of survival.

Having said all this, I still believe in the deep practice of self-understanding and clarity of boundaries and responsibility. A more contemporary take on this comes from the wildly popular student of human nature, Brené Brown. I find her work on vulnerability and shame and courage and belonging to speak more closely to the messy human condition of the self than systems theory sometimes can.

Her book *Braving the Wilderness: The Quest for True Belonging and the Courage to Stand Alone*, speaks well to the challenge that we find ourselves in with religious communities: struggling to balance the self with community. She defines the challenge this way:

> Belonging is the innate human desire to be part of something larger than us. Because this yearning is so primal, we often try to acquire it by fitting in and by seeking approval, which are not only hollow substitutes for belonging, but often barriers to it. Because true belonging only happens when we present our authentic, imperfect selves to the world, our sense of belonging can never be greater than our level of self-acceptance.[10]

Taking the word "BRAVING," she has developed a set of strategies that are, I believe, a great prescription for self-differentiation:

Boundaries: Learning to set, hold, and respect boundaries. The challenge is letting go of being liked and the fear of disappointing people.

Reliability: Learning how to say what we mean and mean what we say. The challenge is not overcommitting and overpromising to please others or prove ourselves.

Accountability: Learning how to step up, be accountable, take responsibility, and issue meaningful apologies when we're wrong. The challenge is letting go of blame and staying out of shame.

Vault: Learning how to keep confidences, to recognize what's ours to share and what's not. The challenge is to stop using gossip, common enemy intimacy, and oversharing as a way to hotwire connection.

Integrity: Learning how to practice our values even when it's uncomfortable and hard. The challenge is choosing courage over comfort in those moments.

Nonjudgment: Learning how to give and receive help. The challenge is letting go of "helper and fixer" as our identity and the source of our self-worth.

Generosity: Learning how to set the boundaries that allow us to be generous in our assumptions about others. The challenge is being honest and clear with others about what's okay and not okay.[11]

Following these practices is not an easy path, but I believe it helps us arrive at a deeper kind of self-differentiation, and Brown offers many tools for getting there.

THE ENNEAGRAM

I often advocate for using the Enneagram personality system as another helpful tool for developing self-understanding and insight. The Enneagram is a model of human typologies detailed in nine primary types. Unlike other personality style methodologies such as Myers-Briggs, the Enneagram does not just stick you into a categorical box and leave you there. It helps you understand your core motivations and offers directions for growth unique to your type. Some say that the theory is based in Sufi thought, and many religious communities have taken it up as a method of spiritual as well as personal growth.[12] While it still designates people as belonging to a particular type, it offers a far more nuanced understanding of the gifts and challenges of each type.

I was introduced to the Enneagram during my second year in ministry when, at the tender age of 27, I was beginning to see that my typical ways of doing things weren't always the best strategies to employ. Let me be more honest: I was hitting a wall that I couldn't talk my way out of, and I couldn't figure out why. A parishioner introduced me to the model and gave me a set of cassette tapes (now that dates me!) of Father Richard Rohr, a Franciscan monk who is greatly responsible for bringing the Enneagram to public attention. I admit to having been skeptical. I couldn't stand the typical tests that brand you forever with categories that have no subtlety. But I was leaving town for a short vacation and needed something to listen to on the drive.

When Rohr got to the type that I immediately recognized as my own, the Eight—often known as the Challenger or the Boss—I found myself listening with tears streaming down my face. How was it possible that he knew so much about me? And, more disturbingly, how could he see all the ways in which my greatest strengths were also my greatest deficits? It was incredibly uncomfortable and humbling. But the more I learned, the more I was able to apply its wisdom to my life and my ministry in two primary ways.

First, I began to identify when I was moving into an unhealthy place, and knew the strategies that would help change that direction. To be more specific, as an Eight, a danger sign for me is when I start to disappear into my head, believing that I can avoid all the messy emotional things by showing people how right I am! But when I do as the Enneagram has taught me, and consciously acknowledge and honor my own and others' emotions, it has *always* been beneficial.

Second, and just as importantly, I began to really grasp the truth that (gasp!) everyone isn't like me! It is an obvious statement that I think few of us really completely integrate. It is so easy to believe that someone is behaving in some way that is difficult for me just because they're trying to mess with me—when, in reality, people act out of entirely different motivations that demand that *I* go the extra mile to try to understand. This requires that I take the time and energy to listen and learn about the other person. As we will see in the next chapter, that is indeed one of the most important steps toward conflict transformation.

I have used this tool with staff members and students, a process always helpful in their own edification, as well as in team-building. But I have also taught it to lay people in workshops. It has the effect of not only helping individuals come to self-understanding, but it also helps to "lower the heat" in a conflicted situation because suddenly people begin to understand the second point above, and they develop greater patience with one another. One important note about this strategy: if you are not well-trained in the Enneagram, it can be dangerous to try to train others. It is a complicated system that can do as much harm as good if not taught well. Contact a local practitioner (most communities have one) or find one online that can help teach it for you.

THE POWER OF A POSITIVE NO

And one last helpful tool: William Ury's excellent book, *The Power of a Positive No*,[13] offers us a very interesting twist on uncovering our values. You may recognize Ury as the partner of Roger Fisher of *Getting to Yes* fame—the subtitle says it all: *Negotiating Agreement without Giving In*.[14] In this more recent book, Ury focuses on our discomfort with saying "No!" Our culture often trains us to believe that *no* has the potential to divide and escalate conflict. Women seem to internalize this message much more intently than men. "No!" seems like the two-year-old response to anything, and we all know how far that gets the two-year-old! But if we are going to learn how to uphold boundaries and set limits on what we can and can't do, we cannot avoid it.

Ury flips the question and asks us to think first about *what we are saying yes to*. Rather than starting with the *no* that can alienate, it helps to be clear about what you *do* value. I teach this method to my staff all the time. In the face of a demanding congregant, it can be far more effective to say, "I really want to do the best job I can on the newsletter, so, I'm sorry, I just can't get to your request right now" than to say, "No, I won't do that!" Just as we've come to realize, it can be hard to surface those values that undergird our decisions. Ury offers us a practice that can take us through that process.

Often the biggest challenge we encounter by understanding ourselves better is that we just don't take the time to do it. Pressures of work and family and who knows what can get in our way. But creating the space and time to engage in some of these practices actually helps alleviate some of the pressure. To return to David Whyte's reflections about feeling besieged:

> Besieged as we are, little wonder that men and women alternate between the dream of a place apart, untouched by the world and then wanting to be wanted again in that aloneness. Besieged or left alone, we seem to live best at the crossroad between irretrievable aloneness and irretrievable belonging, and even better, as a conversation between the two where no choice is available. We are both; other people will never go away and aloneness is both possible and necessary.
>
> Creating a state of aloneness in the besieged everyday may be one of the bravest things individual men and women can do for themselves. "Nel mezzo," in the midst of everything, as Dante said, to be besieged—but beautifully, because we have made a place to stand—in the people and the places and the perplexities we have grown to love, seeing them not now as enemies or forces laying siege, but as if for the first time, as participants in the drama, both familiar and strangely surprising. We find that having people knock on our door is as a much a privilege as it is a burden; that being seen, being recognized and being wanted by the world and having a place in which to receive everyone and everything, is infinitely preferable to its opposite.[15]

Creating a space to stand alone, to learn to understand ourselves, actually allows us to be with others in compassion and acceptance.

Questions for Discussion

- What are the kinds of experiences that "trigger" you? Is there something to which you always become reactive?
- Do you have practices that help you when you become reactive? What are they?
- Is it difficult for you to establish healthy boundaries?
- Do you struggle with saying no? What helps you say no?
- Have you had an experience of a personal epiphany? When you finally realized something about yourself you hadn't been aware of before? What helped you do so?

Chapter Four

From Me to We

Covenantal Dialogue

Only holiness will call people to listen now. And the work of holiness is not about perfection or niceness; it is about belonging, that sense of being in the Presence and through the quality of that belonging, the mild magnetic of implicating others in the Presence. . . . This is not about forging a relationship with a distant God but about the realization that we are already within God.

—John O'Donohue[1]

A former parishioner of mine once said to me: "I trust everyone. I just trust them to be themselves." I remember being shocked at the concept of trusting *everyone*. How could I possibly trust everyone when people so often behave in untrustworthy ways? But I have sat with this wisdom in the many years since it was offered. Perhaps the onus is not on others to behave in ways that I expect? Perhaps one of the obligations is for me to learn more about the other person so that I can know more deeply what to put my trust in.

If the first task in transformation is the obligation to examine my own values, beliefs, and motivations, the second task is surely to seek to understand the other, before too many assumptions are made, before I have walked so far up the ladder that I can't find my way down again.

UNDERSTANDING OUR OWN BIASES

Let us return for a moment to the question of why understanding our-selves is a key component of healthy interactions with others. Richard Rohr says it well:

> Learning how to see our biases is a psychological exercise, but one with immediate theological and social implications. It demands self-knowledge and the crucial need to recognize (1) when we are in denial about our own shadow and capacity for illusion; (2) our capacity to project our own fears and shadows onto other people and groups; (3) our capacity to face and carry our own issues; and (4) the social, institutional, and political implications of not doing this work.[2]

Without developing this understanding, we can get lost in our own righteousness, our own *rightness.* And doing so ends up simply creating resistance in others. Again, this is very hard work to do. It makes our brains work harder than they want to, because it forces us to re-examine the stories that make sense to us, those that follow the pattern of our own assumptions. Jacqui Lewis, senior pastor of Middle Collegiate Church and public theologian, explains it this way:

> We are all wired by what we've experienced to be in search of a story with an ending . . . that feels like it has a completion. And the stories that we gravitate to are the ones that make sense to us, stories that fit, stories that feel like they have continuity, connection to the past, where we've been. . . . Those stories that we will follow are the ones that feel true, feel like they have continuity to our past and that resonate with the trajec-tory of our lives. So, we're looking for the story that doesn't necessarily change our minds; we're actually looking for the story that confirms what's in our minds.[3]

While this is indeed our reflexive response, the result of not explor-ing the validity of our own stories is that we miss out on something important that we may need to learn. We close down opportunities for exploration—our own, most especially.

CONVERSATION AS SPIRITUAL GROWTH

I learned this lesson in a dramatic fashion when I was serving as a district executive. The structure and history of the former district system in the Unitarian Universalist Association defied logic or functionality, and it was constantly a struggle to break down that structure into something more workable for everyone. In one particular moment we were making a proposal to a neighboring district to share staffing as a way of helping them be more financially viable.

My supervisor and I came in to a meeting with that district board with a detailed plan and many explanations for why it made sense. I was raring to go with all the arguments on my side. But my supervisor, wisely, started the meeting by asking all the board participants to talk about what they were experiencing as a result of their former staff having been removed from them. I couldn't believe it. Surely, I thought, we can get down to brass tacks! Why waste all this time by asking how they feel? (Said the Eight to herself.) But I schooled myself in patience and let the process proceed.

What happened next is something that I consider a spiritual growth experience, as well as a valuable lesson in managing complex groups. As the board members talked, they began to see for themselves why their previous structure was untenable. They worked through their grief about their loss, while acknowledging the inadequacy of their former staff. By the end of what felt like a very long day of processing, the board had come to their *own* realization of why our plan should proceed, adding some valuable elements themselves. Everyone felt excited about the future we could now explore together. *This would never have happened if the meeting had proceeded the way I originally conceived.* The board would have been defensive and unable to even process the possibilities of the plan.

I call this a spiritual experience because it was truly faith-affirming to set aside my preconceptions and instead to observe the capacity of others to come to their own answers. I realized that my hubris of believing that I was the only one with the answers cut me off from any appreciation of the capacity of others to have something to teach me that I needed to learn. I also learned something about the fullness of human experience: that feelings of grief or fear of manipulation are just as important to acknowledge as intellectual ideas.

COVENANTAL DIALOGUE

Work like this requires more than just listening skills—though good-
ness knows, listening skills would help. Most of us are woefully un-
trained in them. But what I am addressing here is what is often called
deep listening, or covenantal dialogue. I like the latter term because it
takes us into the realm of spiritual practice. It requires an opening of
our spirits as well as of our minds. As John O'Donohue stated: "Only
holiness will call people to listen now. And the work of holiness is not
about perfection or niceness; it is about belonging."[4]

The humorist Fran Liebowitz said "the opposite of talking isn't listening; the opposite of talking is waiting." Good listening is not just
about letting the other person talk, all the while thinking about what
you are going to say in response! It requires suspending our own assumptions and creating an open space within ourselves that allows us to
truly take in what others are saying. And not just for our own sake: good
listening helps the dialogue partner feel affirmed and acknowledged,
which in turn lowers their barriers and resistance.

Healthy covenantal dialogue asks us to make sure we have heard
correctly what the other person is saying. Repeating back what we
have heard and listening yet again for whether we have it right creates
a space in which others feel that we are taking them and their concerns
seriously. This practice requires a discipline few of us have exercised,
and can sometimes feel false and stilted. Yet, without it, we risk—once
again—traveling up a ladder of inference that the other may never have
intended. It also requires listening for more than just the words people
use. We must notice their feelings as well! Feelings that, as we have
been learning, come across in embodied ways. This is why it is so
dangerous to respond to an emotionally freighted issue through email.
Email lacks the ability to see the whole person, to really gauge the emotional impact of our words as well as to read the emotional landscape of
the other. If necessary, you can write that outraged email to help get it
out of your system. But don't send it!

Once we have done the work of making sure we understand what the
other is saying, it is important to share positive reactions before leaping to concerns or criticism. This is yet another practice that will not
feel intuitive to many of us. There is considerable evidence that we are
hardwired to respond more to the negative than to the positive.[5] We are

back to that pesky amygdala that pays constant attention to danger as a survival strategy. But the good news is that we can retrain our brains by consciously and deliberately looking for the positive in our conversation. Developing this practice in and of itself can be helpful to our own lives, as well as certainly creating opportunities for better outcomes in our conversations.

One of the hang-ups that we often have, that gets in the way of this kind of conversation, is the belief that engaging in it implies that we are in full agreement with the other person. If we waited for full agreement about everything, we may not ever have any conversations! I understand that putting ourselves in the position of engaging with someone with whom we have a deep disagreement can feel like we are rewarding them. But again, there exists the possibility that we may learn something from the conversation! And the act of engaging in dialogue of this sort in and of itself signals to the other that the relationship is still valuable, and will, perhaps, lower their defensiveness.

In *High Conflict: Why We Get Trapped and How We Get Out*, Amanda Ripley explores this:

> People do escape high conflict. Individuals—even entire communities— find ways to short-circuit the feedback loops of conflict. They don't suddenly agree, and this is important: they don't surrender their beliefs. Nor do they defect, switching from one position to the opposite extreme.
>
> Instead, they do something much more interesting: they become capable of comprehending that with which they still disagree. Like someone who learns a second language, they start to hear the other side without compromising their own beliefs. And that changes everything. Curiosity returns. Humanity revives. IQs go back up. Conflict becomes necessary and good, instead of just draining.[6]

Let me stipulate at this point that there are, indeed, times when it simply isn't safe to be in conversation with someone with whom you are in conflict. If you feel physically or psychologically threatened, there is no obligation for you to stay in the conversation.

Ramon is a minister who is quite skilled in establishing complex governance systems for larger congregations. He was called to a church that had struggled for years in this arena, and based on his conversations with the search committee, he believed that everyone in the church shared the desire to streamline decision-making. Unfortunately, this streamlining meant doing away with committees that had been important sources of engagement for some leaders. They felt their work was now disregarded and undervalued. Two such leaders happened to be the chair and vice-chair of the board, and they began to block and undermine Ramon as he tried to put new structures in place. He thought that they would eventually settle down and come to see the wisdom of his approach. But instead, they started fomenting unrest in the larger congregation. A wise elder in the church helped Ramon see that he needed to back up and truly listen to the chair and vice chair. After a long and challenging conversation in which he was able to reflect back to them a much deeper understanding of their concerns, they were able to move forward together. Much more slowly than Ramon had hoped! But with far greater chance of success.

In the previous chapter on systems, we talked about how process is often far more important than content, but content—particularly *how we present* content—can be important as well.

POSITIONS AND INTERESTS

Again, when we are talking about the need to be affirming and offer some positive responses in a conversation, this does not mean that you can't be clear about your own perspective and how that differs from the other. The question is *how* you frame your ideas. I say *ideas* here rather than your *position* for a deliberate reason. Remember our ladder of inference: taking a position puts us very high up on that ladder. That doesn't mean you can't have opinions. But your opinions are best presented when they are accompanied by the *interests and values* that inform your position.

For example, saying something like, "I think the congregation needs to build a new annex," without any explication of your thinking process, can just invite opposition. If, however, you can say, "I think it is important for us to create an inviting space for families to engage with the congregation and I'm concerned that our current space may not allow us to do that," an invitation to dialogue about values occurs. *Positions* polarize; *interests* create a greater opportunity for connection and to find common ground. Our interests are the needs, desires, concerns, and fears that motivate us. These are more likely to be shared by the other and will help them understand why you have come to the position that you have. In essence, you are walking yourself down your ladder by asking yourself things such as "Why is this so important to me?" and "What are the assumptions that got me to this place that may not be the same as others?"

INQUIRY AND ADVOCACY

Once the dialogue has been established on this basis, it is perfectly fine for you to go ahead and advocate for a particular decision or action. You have already been engaging in respectful inquiry that has hopefully taught you something about the interests the other shares, and you can build on those common interests to explain why you have come to the decision or opinion that you have. Engaging in conversations without *inquiry* is most likely to create defensiveness and polarization. But if you are a leader in the congregation, it is incumbent upon you to ultimately make a decision. If you get lost in *only* affirming feelings and feel that you have to get to a place where everyone agrees, you are abdicating your leadership role. But, as is hopefully obvious by now, a group is more likely to accept and support your decision when the members have felt fully listened to by you.

Jackson is the administrator of a congregation that makes a great deal of money renting out its beautiful building and grounds for weddings. The wedding couples are often not members of the church, so they don't always understand the complexity of church concerns. At one point it became clear that the roof of the main chapel of the church was in dire need of repair. Jackson was put in the uncomfortable position of having to tell wedding couples who had already booked the chapel that the building would be unusable. The church decided to offer to provide tents and other kinds of outdoor amenities to make up for this change. For most couples this seemed to be a reasonable concession. For one particular couple it was far more problematic. They began to demand concession after concession. Jackson, whose main concern was the financial stability of the church, reacted with resistance and offered technical explanations of why they couldn't do what the couple wished. Finally a member of the board caught on to what was happening. Jackson, who is White, didn't understand the cultural nuances of the concerns shared by the couple, who are Chinese. The Chinese member of the board explained that in his culture, weddings are elaborate and often involve difficult relational issues. By focusing on the technical reasons why the change had to be made, rather than offering a clear apology and listening deeply to the complexities of the concerns, Jackson made a difficult situation worse.

If all of this sounds stilted and uncomfortable, that's because it is! As I said, we have not been trained to engage in conversations this way. It will take practice, and you will make mistakes along the way. But speaking from my own personal experience, I can attest to how much more helpful my conversations have been when I don't assert my opinions and positions first. It is worth the effort. At some point I realized that *being right* was not always the point, no matter how convinced I was of my righteousness! *Being effective,* by opening a space for mutual learning, has gotten me much further in life and, most importantly, made me a better person and a better minister.

Exercise

1. Describe to a listening partner an experience of conflict you have had. Try to convey your interests and feelings about the experience, as well as any positions you may have taken.
2. The listening partner then reflects back to the speaker what they have heard and checks to see if they got it right.
3. Switch positions.

Chapter Five

Congregational Systems

First set the warp,
the plain, stable threads
that hold the pattern in place—
the infrastructure of joy,
the girders that hold up all we build
of meaning, or justice, or peace.
Use strong threads left
by those who have gone before.
Only then pick up the weft,
the colored thread that you will use
to weave according to your plan.
Choose carefully—this is what
the world will see, each tiny act
that builds the bright pattern
of your life. Yes, the threads
will tangle or knot or fray,
and the flaws will show.
Oh well. Tuck in the ends
as best you can and start again.
This is not the time to stop your weaving.
So much is pulling at the great design.

—Lynn Ungar[1]

Now that we have begun exploring the multiple dimensions of the self in relationship to conflict, and journeyed through the dynamics of healthy conversations, we can turn our attention more fully to how this can play out in congregational life.

CONGREGATIONS AS SYSTEMS

Congregations are more than just the sum of their parts, and more complicated than just a collection of interlocking relationships. When I worked at our denominational headquarters, I would often be approached by my colleagues who didn't have a lot of practical experience in congregations. "How do we communicate with the congregations?" they would ask in frustration. And I would answer, adding to their frustration, "Which congregation do you mean? The membership as it exists now? The clergy, the current lay leadership?" At least in my system of congregational polity, there is no single *thing* called a congregation. Ministers come and they go. Lay leaders come and go even more rapidly, even if they stay active in the congregation. New people join and frustrated people leave and, sadly, beloved members die. Congregations are living, breathing organisms that change and grow (or shrink).

People forget this reality at their peril. Again, in my role at our headquarters, I could often tell when people began their position, just by their attitude toward the organization. It is human nature to assume that the organization we are in now is just the same as when we started with it. While this is a natural phenomenon, it needs to be taken out and reexamined periodically. For example, the district executive who began in 2001 when budgets were generous and bold new initiatives were possible can be frustrated and angry at the process of budget cutting that happened in 2009 after the great recession. Even though they may logically know that times have changed, it is hard for them not to feel like their work isn't valued when their staff are let go or their initiatives denied.

Similarly, in congregations, the congregation a person joined is the one that they still interact with in their heads. "We never used to have trouble recruiting religious education teachers. There must be a problem with the RE director." Add to this dynamic the deeply held value systems of one generation that are very different from those of the next generation. Gil Rendle explores this challenge in his book, *The*

Multigenerational Congregation.[2] The woman in her 70s who used to volunteer at the church three days a week looks at the woman in her 40s juggling children and career who barely has time for a committee meeting once a month and thinks "bad member," even if unconsciously. I once had an elderly woman who had been a part of the congregation for decades say to me: "We never used to have presents and praise for outgoing leadership. They just knew it was their job and got on with it!" Clearly it wasn't the case that she didn't appreciate the current leadership. It was just a practice that seemed superfluous to her. And newer, younger members clearly want to feel rewarded for the work that often takes them away from their families or their career.

Congregations change all the time. *And* it is also true that every congregation has a particular kind of system that persists over time. Call it a personality, formed by a multitude of experiences and people. This is where family systems theory comes back into play in a helpful way. Systems theory teaches us that *systems* are always more powerful than *individuals*. You can change the players, but the system will remain in place.

For example, as an interim minister I work with congregations who have said goodbye to a previous minister. These ministers may have been revered or reviled (and sometimes both!), but a congregation needs to do the work of uncovering its identity beyond that of the minister. I can always tell when congregations haven't really done this interim processing work. They either end up calling a new minister who is almost exactly like the previous minister (even when that minister was reviled!) or, conversely, a minister who is almost exactly the opposite (even when the minister was beloved). Either way, the congregational *system* is making a *reactive* decision, not a responsive and thoughtful decision. This is not because the search committees didn't do their job right. It is because the system demanded of them (entirely subconsciously) a particular kind of minister.

If that sounds too mystical for you, let me offer a different example. In my first settled parish I arrived to find a treasurer who was the bane of everyone's existence. He kept the church books and computer files at home (this was way before the cloud existed!) and wouldn't let others see them. He would issue paychecks for staff, only if the amount of income that month equaled or exceeded the payroll. He would personally nix much-needed improvement projects and refuse to pay for them, even if they had been approved by the board. He resisted my attendance at finance committee meetings—"don't you worry your pretty head about these numbers, Reverend." Because he worked tirelessly, and because, frankly, people were afraid of challenging him, the leadership let him stay in place. It took all of my political efforts to finally manage to dislodge him two years after my arrival. I recruited the nicest, most amenable person on the finance committee that I could find to take his place. Relief at last! Within only a few months, my nice new recruit was behaving in almost identical ways to the previous treasurer. The system had reasserted itself, even to the extent that it changed the personality of the person in that position. Clearly, there was deeply embedded anxiety about money in the system, anxiety that ended up being acted out by the person serving as treasurer.

The lesson here is not that congregational systems are immutable. They can indeed change. But systems can't be changed by intellectually identifying the issues, or changing the players. Change requires deeply excavating sometimes painful experiences and paying attention to systemic patterns that manifest over and over again.

An interim colleague recently told me a story about a congregation she served that absolutely refused to take on what my denomination calls becoming a "Welcoming Congregation"—a process that requires the congregation to examine their assumptions and prejudices (even unconscious) that have excluded LGBTQ people in the past and institute practices to be more openly welcoming. It is helpful to note that almost *all* of our Unitarian Universalist congregations have gone through this process—not without pain and struggle, but they engaged with it and came out the other side. When my colleague began to pry through the layers of issues around this particular congregation's reluctance, she discovered that it wasn't necessarily that they were more homophobic than any other congregation. What finally surfaced was this story: several years before, the members held a large congregational meeting about the welcoming congregation process in which two people ended up in a shouting and then shoving match. This traumatizing experience made them reluctant to take up the issue again. Once my colleague learned about this history, she began to help them discern that the issue was really about how to have conversations about difficult subjects. She helped convince the members that it is possible! She introduced the idea of relational covenants, which they began to practice, and they are now a Welcoming Congregation.

I could go on about system dynamics, but that would take us slightly off course. At this point, however, I want to highlight a core concept in systems ideology that relates to our work in previous chapters: no one can change a system by trying to ask a system to change, and certainly not by demanding it. But, as Gil Rendle notes in the foreword to this book, one can help shift a system by refusing to act as the system dictates. In other words, you can't change the system but you can change yourself, which ends up changing the system! This requires all the skills of self-awareness that I outlined in chapter 3. It is not work for the faint of heart, but it has great power.

SYSTEMIC ANXIETY

For some congregations, the congregational system chugs along beneath the surface without causing too much distress. People may joke about "we just don't do things like that around here," but it doesn't cause great conflict. But in congregations where unresolved conflicts crop up in unexpected ways, there is more overt systemic anxiety.

You can tell an anxious system by these typical signs:

- There is a general lack of boundaries. Gossip flies and people feel pressured to "go along to get along."
- There is a pattern of scapegoating: blaming the minister or a lay leader or some other party for whatever is causing the distress.
- The problem gets stuck on repeat—it keeps happening over and over again, perhaps with different players or different details, but the same general problem never gets resolved.
- People get focused on technical fixes: let's change the bylaws. Let's change the policies. Let's change whatever is less emotionally taxing that keeps us from having to confront the deeper emotional issues involved.
- The leadership seems incapable of acting. They may all be good and competent people, but they can't seem to make the big decisions.

- There is a general lack of imagination or creativity. "We've always done it this way" becomes gospel, and woe betide the person who tries to do things differently.

When these signs are apparent, you know there will be significant systemic work to do, and conflicts are bound to come up in unhealthy ways.

A congregation I once consulted with had a history of having ministers that many people were greatly dissatisfied with, but they let these ministers stay in place well past their ability to effectively function. A constant refrain I heard from lay people was, "The board just doesn't act!" I began to ask the question: "Do you actually *empower* the board to act?" They then started looking at the ways in which they had inadvertently structured leadership in their bylaws that undermined the authority of the board, as well as how the congregation had a history of electing leaders that weren't terribly decisive. They began to see that they had set up a system that was almost incapable of letting go of a minister until it got to the most dysfunctional place.

Irene served a church that began as a small family-sized congregation. In her first five years of ministry the church started to grow to the point that they needed to build a new building to accommodate all the new people. The congregation successfully raised the necessary money, and Irene went off to take a well-deserved sabbatical. When she returned, she found that the leadership had brought in a new president, Nathan, whom members didn't know very well. Almost immediately Nathan began to create conflicts with the building committee, insisting that they couldn't start building until all the money was in hand. Irene thought it best to try to keep this conflict out of the knowledge of the whole congregation as she worried it might undermine their growth efforts. Finally, the leadership removed Nathan from his position and, infuriated, he wrote a letter to the whole congregation alleging financial malfeasance and bullying behavior from Irene. They ended up calling a congregational meeting in which people asked Nathan for the evidence of his charges, and he had none. And everyone knew that Irene was the furthest thing from a bully you could imagine! The congregation underwent healthy congregation training and established teams to help hold people to their covenantal agreements. By the time the congregation grew to such a size as to require yet another new building, the transition was made without major conflicts erupting.

It would be easy to label this conflict as the fault of Nathan and his dysfunctional behavior. But it is important to understand that there was sufficient systemic anxiety brewing in the congregation about growth and change, and that he was able to maintain his position for some time. By trying to hide the conflict, it only became more toxic and destructive. But finally airing the issues and concerns helped the congregation see the dynamics at play, and learning and establishing new behavioral agreements helped them shift the system to a much healthier place that could withstand conflict even in the midst of considerable growth and change.

PAYING ATTENTION

A question that may be coming to mind is, How does one assess their congregational system? When you are an integral part of the system, it can be like the proverbial fish who can't name the water it swims in. One method that may sound rather simplistic is to take note of *what you do, rather than what you say.* When I am working with staff members who feel particularly stuck and question whether they're working in alignment with their job description, I ask them simply to take note of what they spend their time doing in a week. At the end of the week, we go over the list. Often what we find is that they are spending far more time on things that are really not their priority. We talk about why that is and whether the job description needs to change, or, how to let go of some of the expectations that were taking them off track. Quite often it happens because a lay leader makes a demand to which the staff doesn't know how to say no.

The same is true of congregational life. What do you actually spend most of your time doing? You may have a beautifully worded and inspiring mission statement, but if you actually spend most of your time hashing out policies and procedures, then that has become your *lived* mission, whether you intended it or not. In his book, *Paying Attention,*[3] Gary Peluso-Verdend explicates the process of aligning our practices with our purpose. This sounds easier than it is. Often the things a

congregation obsesses over are symptoms of a past trauma or a simmering conflict that hasn't yet risen to the surface.

> That is the case when we attend to symptoms rather than finding and at-
> tending to the systemic conflicts. We shovel away the droppings from the
> elephant in the room or spray air fresheners but either ignore the elephant
> or, if we are unaware of the elephant, hardly wonder why we spend so
> much time cleaning and freshening.[4]

Once we start seeing what we are giving our attention to, we can
then ask two important questions: (1) Does this relate to an unresolved
conflict or trauma that needs to be uncovered? And (2) Is this really the
best way to live out our mission?

Why do we attend to things that are not critical to our mission? Gil
Rendle explains that

> organizations and their leaders will collude to give attention to those
> things that won't embarrass them. It is embarrassing to stumble about in
> the dark of not knowing. It therefore becomes much more tempting to go
> to those places where the "light" of familiar questions and known answers
> offers a sense of progress even when, intuitively, people know that they
> are searching in the wrong spot. So leaders encourage people to double
> down on efforts that have lost their effectiveness.[5]

A large congregation that had been strong and vital began to struggle
to maintain its vitality. People were leaving leadership positions and
a beloved minister decided to retire, leaving the leadership wondering
what had gone wrong. An interim minister came in and started observ-
ing some interesting dynamics. The congregation had recently decided
to adopt a policy governance style of working, which required the
minister to write reams of monitoring reports, and took time away from
other important ministerial duties. The church had also recently sold a
piece of property, which created a substantial new endowment. It was
discovered that there were serious structural issues in the religious education building that required immediate repair, so the leadership asked
whether the new endowment could be tapped for this necessary work.
But the trustees who oversaw the account refused to spend from it, arguing for a fiscally conservative approach. The interim minister was able
to hold up a mirror to these behaviors and ask if that was really what the
congregation wanted to be doing. Were detailed reports really what they

wanted the minister to focus on? Was saving and holding on to money instead of providing a safe space for religious exploration to occur really the purpose of endowments? A new and deeper conversation about the mission of the congregation ensued, and vitality began to revive.

CONGREGATIONAL TIMELINE

Another process that can help assess your system is to do a timeline exercise. Interim ministers use this tool all the time to help uncover patterns and important stories from the past that have helped form the congregation's identity. This is an exercise best done with as many people participating as possible. There are often hidden stories that emerge from people who may not be involved in leadership. Here is how I conduct the process:

- Create a timeline with three columns. The first column is the name and tenure of the minister. The second column is for identifying the issues and significant experiences of the congregation during that time. The third column names what was happening in the larger community or world. I organize this around ministries not because the minister is the most important person, but more to create a way to identify eras.
- Beginning with the earliest ministry, ask participants to fill in the second column. If it is a relatively small group, this is best done by having people call things out. If the group is too large for that, it may be necessary for people to fill out sticky notes that they can come up and review once everyone has added theirs.
- Then go through the same process for the third column, asking them to identify the larger context. It's important to go through each column for each ministry before moving on to the next. If the earliest ministries took place before anyone present was alive, you can have people offer stories that they have heard about that time.

The point of this process is *not* to tell a single, seamless story about the congregation. Inevitably there will be people who describe minister X as the greatest preacher ever, and others who describe that same minister as boring and disengaged. That's okay! It's helpful for people to see that it is possible to have different perspectives that can still live with one another.

When, however, those stories become wildly divergent from one another, you may have identified a time of conflict and trauma that is worth exploring. Often when I do this exercise a bombshell will be dropped, such as "Minister Y in 1945 was arrested for pedophilia." Sometimes those bombshells are dropped by the quiet elderly woman in the back that few people pay attention to. Do not ignore these bombshells! They tell you something very important about traumas that have entered the system that are still being played out, even if the actual incident is almost completely forgotten.

I include the third column of understanding the larger context of each ministry because all too often a congregation can get lost inside of itself, forgetting that important things happening outside can have their own impact. In particular you will find that traumas in the larger culture (war, recession, terrorism) will be acted out within the congregation as well. I know many a congregation that has split over whether to support a war, or to engage in controversial political issues. Ministry and congregational life do not take place in a vacuum.

TRIANGLES

An important element of congregational systems that needs to be attended to is the concept of triangles. As I noted earlier, a congregation as a whole is greater than its parts. But, having said that, I will also note that one of the building blocks of congregational systems is triangles. We hear all the time about how we should avoid triangulation, but I think that triangles are often misunderstood as always being bad. In fact, triangles are a natural way for human beings to relate to one another. One-on-one interactions can often be intense, as noted in the previous chapter, and so it often helps to distribute anxiety by inviting another into conversation and relationship. Such triangles often give us healthy ways to check our assumptions.

Triangles become unhealthy, however, when they are used as a means to manipulate another. For example, if I am talking with Mary to help me sort out my frustrations with Cynthia, that can be a healthy triangle because Mary may help me understand something I might have missed about Cynthia. If, however, I am talking with Mary about Cynthia, *and then I ask Mary to go sort out my problems with Cynthia*, I am engaging in an unhealthy practice. If you think about it, there is no way that Mary can fully represent my issues to Cynthia, because *she isn't me*. Further, there is no way for Cynthia to really sort things out with me, because I have cut myself out of the triangle.

Andre was a music minister who had been working in a congregation for decades. He was incredibly popular with many participants in the music program. But from a staff perspective he was extremely difficult to work with. He often didn't inform the staff about important programs until close to the time they occurred, which made it hard to appropriately plan and support those efforts. When Jose arrived as a new minister, he started calling out these behaviors and asking for changes in how Andre operated. Andre quit in a great huff, and organized private meetings of people in the music program in which he aired his sense of hurt and betrayal. Members of the program began arriving at Jose's door asking that he "fix" the problems and work to bring Andre back. At this point Andre refused to engage with the church so there was no opportunity to try to work through the disputes, even had Jose wanted to. Many people left the music program and Jose continued to be pressured to resolve the problems with Andre. The music program began to fall apart, and Jose's ministry was imperiled from the beginning.

When unhealthy triangles such as this abound in a congregational system, we end up with many of the signs of anxiety: secrets, gossiping, and blaming spread like wildfire, fanning the flames of dysfunction, with no opportunity to bring healing waters to bear.

Every congregation will have its traumas and conflicts and challenges. The question will be how to find a way to use these as learning experiences rather than trying to brush them under the rug or fight about them, over and over again, in a never-ending cycle.

CYCLES OF CONFLICT IN CONGREGATIONAL LIFE

An incredibly helpful tool can help us see the dynamics and cycles of conflict in the life of the congregation. It was developed by Adam Curle and adapted by John Paul Lederach to illustrate different manifestations of conflict (figure 5.1).[6]

The Curle Diagram

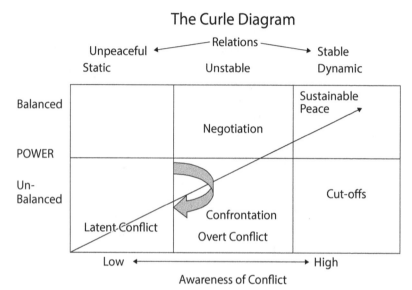

Figure 5.1.   **The Curle diagram.** *Developed by Adam Curle and adapted by John Paul Lederach.*

Congregations often linger in the lower-left box of latent conflict. The conflict exists, but few people really want to talk about it. You'll notice that even though the conflict is latent, the relations are not peaceful—they are static and stuck. Much like Irene's congregation described before, the attempt to keep things under wraps means there is no opportunity to really work through the issues.

Something then happens to force the conflict out into the open and overt conflict comes to the fore (Nathan's letter to the congregation). At this point a congregation can make several different choices as to how to deal with the conflict. Confrontation could ensue, with parties battling it out with each other in damaging ways. Or, the congregation could choose to open a way to negotiation, with a transparent process and an opportunity for all to be heard. (We will discuss strategies for this move in a subsequent chapter.) Or, the confrontations can lead to such distress that people get ejected from or leave the congregation (in systems parlance, cut-offs occur). This includes the kind of blaming and scapegoating practices named above, and it almost always involves some very unhealthy triangles such as what Andre helped create. An uneasy peace may be restored, but there is no opportunity to process and learn from the conflict.

Ultimately, if the congregation learns to engage in open and healthy processes as did Irene's church, it can get to what Curle calls "sustainable peace." I find this terminology not terribly helpful, for it implies an absence of conflict. But the idea is that conflicts inevitably arise and can then be processed in healthy, open, and continuous ways.

You'll see that the vertical axis on the table indicates the level of power balance or imbalance. This can be a complicated concept, and some people interpret this to mean that everyone needs to have the same level of power. Such a utopian situation has never existed in my experience! Nor would I necessarily want it to. Leadership is required (both lay and ministerial) to help move a congregation along. But a healthy balance of power would mean that processes are transparent and that everyone can feel included in appropriate ways.

WHAT DOESN'T WORK

We've all been there, desperately searching for some way to quell the discord. Surely, if we just have a big congregational meeting, people will start to see reason! Or, let's survey everyone anonymously just so that we know where people stand. Or, we can hold a hearing where people on opposite sides can present their arguments and see who prevails. I've seen all these strategies, and have even employed some of them, and I rarely see them work. Why?

Given what we have been exploring about effective communication and covenantal dialogue, we can start to take apart these methods and see their flaws. What happens at large congregational meetings? The most opinionated people end up dominating the conversation, while the introverted or the conflict-phobic people shiver in their pews, not daring to say a word. As we have noted, amygdala stimulation is contagious. If we see other people up in arms, we think that we should be at least on guard; and there goes almost anyone's chance to think reflectively and creatively. In chapter 1, I tell the story of a disastrous congregational meeting at which I was inadvertently spit on! Spitting aside, it didn't help the situation because it just created an opportunity for those who were most upset to take center stage.

I used to wonder why so many congregational conflicts centered around music personnel. But the more I learned about our subliminal emotional responses, the more I began to see why this would be the case. When people are engaged in the communal act of making music, it is a powerful spiritual experience. The boundaries between us fade and we feel a part of something larger than ourselves. If fear can be contagious, so too can joy and sorrow. These experiences are related to the mammalian parts of the brain and often operate below the surface of consciousness. So, if a board removes a music director, the conveyor of all of those subliminally powerful experiences, it can feel akin to ripping a baby out of arms. Given this, why would we think a congregational meeting focused on trying to convey facts and decisions could ever satisfy these deeply emotional concerns?

An exception to this caution against large congregational meetings would be the kind of meetings related to disclosing misconduct, which I will describe in the next chapter. In that case, it is important for people to feel like everyone has access to the same information at the same time, and to hear it verbally, rather than just reading it in a newsletter or email. It is essential for these meetings to be highly structured and facilitated by people skilled in establishing a tone of covenantal conversation.

Let's turn now to surveys. Isn't it a good idea to find some way to learn about how everyone is feeling? And given that we are talking about difficult issues, we should be sure to make the survey confidential so that everyone will participate! What could go wrong? Think about what we are asking people to do: reflect on an issue of deep concern, probably one that is emotionally laden, and represent that concern by choosing a multiple-choice answer. Or fill in an empty line that gives you 50 characters to respond. And who is most likely to answer this survey? Those with the most definite opinions, of course! And because it is confidential, people will feel free to let fly with their judgments and accusations that have layer upon layer of assumptions built into them.

Often these surveys are employed to gather evidence for why a minister or staff person should be let go. But rarely are the questions put that baldly. Instead, people are asked to reflect on things such as the "quality of worship." Is it possible to come up with a uniform understanding of what makes for quality worship that can be represented in a multiple-choice question? The person who is the target of this survey has to go through the tortuous process of reading all the responses that take apart the work they have dedicated their life and soul to for years. At this point, the relationship with said staff person is broken beyond repair. And because the survey is confidential, there is no way to probe deeper to understand why a person responded as they did. The hurt radiates out to supporters and makes the detractors feel smug and righteous. How can deep learning result from this?

Surveys can be helpful tools in congregations—but only surveys about objective issues, such as choosing among the colors being considered for the new carpeting in the sanctuary. Even in this case you can see that emotion could play a role! But, if followed up by open conversation, it can help people recognize when they might hold a minority opinion and be willing to cede to the majority.

And lastly, we can look at "hearings." It should be obvious by now that asking people to engage in a debate will only result in positions becoming more entrenched, and a nuanced conversation about the interests that inform them gets lost along the way.

What we are in search of is a way to *lower* the anxiety in the system, creating opportunities for dialogue rather than discussion, and hopefully engaging our most creative selves. A perfect methodology will not accomplish this. You must take the time to build the skills necessary for this work within the community itself. As congregational consultant David Brubaker says:

> We must earn the right to make change. We can only change what we first love. There are seasons when the leadership, structure, or culture of a congregation must change—at least if the congregation desires a healthy future. But successful change agents know that before they can make change, they must first earn the right to do so by building trusting relationships through listening. Congregational members can intuitively sense whether a leader is operating out of love for the congregation and its people or from ego-driven motives.[7]

We will explore more effective strategies for change in part 2 of the book, but I think it is important to name the unique dynamics of what happens when a congregation experiences misconduct. We will turn to this in the next chapter.

Questions for Discussion

- Can you describe periods of significant trauma in the congregation's history? Are there open and honest conversations about what happened?
- Do you feel like you are living out the congregation's expressed mission? What seems to take up most of your time?
- Are there issues that seem to come up over and over again that never get resolved?

Exercise

In small groups, take a particular conflict in your congregation's history and map it onto the Curle diagram. Was it latent for a time? Was there an explosive period? Did we learn how to create opportunities for negotiation? Were there cut-offs that occurred? What did we learn from it?

Chapter Six

The Repercussions of Misconduct

The church exists, in part, to remember—to rescue from a vast silence the stories that might not otherwise be heard, to ask questions
that might not elsewhere be asked, to celebrate victories and mourn
losses that might otherwise be forgotten, to bless what might go un-
blessed. This remembering, this naming of truth, the consecration of
stories forgotten, forbidden, and hidden, both terrible and beautiful,
is the sacrament of the living word.

—Victoria Safford[1]

When I served on district staff (the middle adjudicatory of the UUA),
my colleagues and I used to talk about how we could recognize a congregation that experienced misconduct just by their behavior, without
even knowing the story of the misconduct. There were patterns of
unhealthy conflict among members, a revolving door of ministers that
were generally blamed for anything that went wrong, a stuckness that
inhibited any real growth or change—in general, a failure to thrive.
Unfortunately, we found this pattern all too often.

Ministerial misconduct (or misconduct by other staff or a prominent
lay leader) can have profound effects on a congregational system, and
as such, deserves a short chapter on its own.

WHAT IS MISCONDUCT?

In her very helpful book, *Wholeness after Betrayal*, Robin Hammeal-Urban offers this clear definition of misconduct:

> At its core, congregational misconduct is a betrayal of trust by a leader who puts his or her needs before those of the people to whom he or she ministers. In essence, the leader abuses the power bestowed by virtue of holding a position of leadership in a church. The opportunity to commit congregational misconduct arises from this trust. The trusted leader can be an ordained or a lay minister.[2]

Because of the tremendous trust that people place in their clergy and leaders, the impact of misconduct affects far more than just the individual people involved at a particular time. It reverberates throughout the system and over time—even for people who have no idea that it happened. If the congregation has been impeded in its ability to process the trauma in a healthy way, patterns of secrecy, of mistrust, and of stifling conversation begin to be a part of the congregation's DNA.

Congregational misconduct expert, Deborah Pope-Lance, describes it this way:

> In all emotional systems, the attitudes and behaviors of leaders—whether fathers or mothers, clergy or laity—powerfully structure and restructure the system. Leaders' interactions are patterned and repeated, and thereafter come to regulate all of a system's interactions. . . . In congregations where a minister commonly makes unilateral decisions or dismisses or ignores others' input, congregants may come to tolerate or exhibit this same behavior. Long after a minister departs, the pattern of interactions persists, pervading the culture of the congregation and regulating the dynamics of all relationships.[3]

As Pope-Lance makes clear, the misconduct need not be sexual to still have impact on a system.

WHY IS IT SO DIFFICULT?

Let's think about why misconduct has such a dramatic impact on a system. In every congregation, people have very different experiences of their minister. Most of the time these differences can coexist as long as most people are getting their needs met in a healthy way. But when ministers violate the deep trust people place in them, that natural variety of response comes to the surface in more destructive ways. There will be the people who refuse to believe their beloved minister is capable of such behavior. There will be those who may believe it but don't think it is serious enough to be cause for dramatic action. The conflict-phobic people will run and hide, and the anxious will spray their anxiety over everything. Unfortunately, victims of the abuse are often not believed or are scapegoated for all the trouble they have "caused," and their stories and concerns and healing go ignored.

Samuel was a newly ordained minister who had been called as an associate to serve a large and vibrant congregation. The senior minister, Ken, was, by most accounts, beloved. Samuel appreciated working with Ken and learned a great deal in his first four years. In his fifth year, Ken decided to retire, and the congregation decided to elevate Samuel to the senior minister position. Almost immediately a crisis started to emerge. It was revealed that the popular music director, Sydney, had been having an affair with a married woman in the choir. Evidently Ken knew about this but didn't do anything to address it. As the investigation got underway, more incidents of Sydney's misconduct came to light, with each woman believing that they were the only one. Samuel and the board decided that they had to make this public, and took action to fire Sydney.

There was a firestorm in response, with people taking positions all across the spectrum. Some minimized the behavior and demanded Sydney's reinstatement. Others wanted to know every detail of the stories, which, of course, could not be shared. Still others simply didn't believe it. The board and Samuel held steady and were able to help the congregation move forward with a multitude of very difficult meetings, small and large. Just as they thought the worst had passed, another woman came to the board with a letter that made it clear that Ken, the beloved former senior minister, had also been engaging in an affair. Again, after investigation and much deliberation and prayer, the board and Samuel revealed this new level of misconduct to the congregation.

Once again, a firestorm of even greater dimension occurred. Long-standing friendships were disrupted, beloved members of the church left for good. But board members dedicated themselves to constantly ask: What would serve the *mission* of our congregation, not just our *members*? In so doing, they held a space for themselves, and the congregation, to engage in deep learning about the relationship of a congregation to its ministry, and how to take responsibility for its health. As Safford says so beautifully, "This remembering, this naming of truth, the consecration of stories forgotten, forbidden, and hidden, both terrible and beautiful, is the sacrament of the living word."[4] This work can indeed become sacramental when done prayerfully and intentionally.

Unfortunately, it is not unusual to see multiple cases of misconduct within a congregation like that just described. Typically, a system has grown up around the misbehavior, allowing it to be secret and having few mechanisms for accountability, thereby creating space for someone else to misbehave. Once this board had the courage to expose the multiple levels of abuse, the opportunity for healing helped break open the old system and allow for new learning and growth, which included holding healthy boundaries and systems of accountability.

In cases of sexual misconduct, it is easy to focus on the sexualized relationship as the most damaging thing that happened, but often there are far wider consequences.

Another large and vibrant congregation called a new minister whom they thought would take them to the next level of growth and vitality. Sebastian was extremely charismatic and quickly developed a devoted following. But some were suspicious of him from the beginning. He clearly had people he liked and those he didn't. Those in the "didn't" category got very little attention from him. Anyone who questioned Sebastian was quickly shut down by the leaders he maneuvered into place. The split began to grow wider. As one prominent leader said, "It was like being in a family with divorcing parents. Some people expected that we support the minister regardless, and others felt like their concerns and critiques were silenced, and each group really didn't feel like they could talk to the other."

After a few years it became known to the leadership that there was evidence of financial malfeasance by Sebastian. Then concerns about his treatment of staff surfaced. Just as this was being absorbed, several charges of sexual misconduct were brought. The board finally acted and fired Sebastian, who promptly threatened to sue the board for unfair termination. Because of the legal issues involved, the board did not feel able to reveal details to the congregation, only that there were allegations of misconduct, without specifying what kind. Again, similar to the previous story, the subsequent uproar from the congregation threatened to overwhelm everyone. Eventually the denominational body conducted its own investigation and Sebastian was removed from the ministry. That allowed the board to be more transparent about the reasons for his dismissal, and most people began to come around to the propriety of their actions.

What this story reveals is that the impact of the misconduct was not just about the sexualized relationships with particular congregants. What became apparent was a pattern of emotional manipulation that the minister could use to pit people against each other and rally his supporters. He knew how to prey upon people who were vulnerable and groom them emotionally and spiritually to become dependent on him and his good regard. After his abuse was revealed, it made these supporters question their own judgment in extremely painful ways, and wonder whether the praise he heaped on them was false. Even after the misconduct became public, some people still didn't understand why it was such a big problem. They would frame it as "just an affair," making those who understood its impact feel isolated and unheard.

LEGAL CONSTRAINTS

The congregation just described was advantaged (a relative term!) by the action of the denomination's investigation and subsequent decision to remove Sebastian from ministry, because the leadership felt like the details could be safely discussed. But often, congregational leadership ties itself into knots over whether and how and when to talk about the issues with the whole congregation. Fears about the legality of the exposure, as well as hesitance to open up the emotional explosion that can occur, can make a body want to hide the misconduct. The congregation can sense that there are issues, but the secrecy becomes toxic.

I want to acknowledge here that the legal issues of disclosure are indeed complex and daunting. Often congregational leadership bodies are worried that they will be held legally liable if someone brings suit against them. The lawyers who are consulted for advice understand their role as first and foremost to protect the congregation and consequently urge the most cautious, and therefore the least transparent, of actions.

I don't blame leadership for being concerned. The reality is, however, that very few congregations are successfully sued for wrongful dismissal or libel. It is essential to get legal advice in such instances, but it is most helpful to find attorneys who understand religious employment law, if possible. Such lawyers make the argument that the freedom of religion, as accorded by the Constitution, protects a congregation that can show that it is acting out of spiritual and religious duty.

If your congregation is confronting a current allegation of misconduct, I highly recommend following the processes outlined by Robin Hammeal-Urban referenced above. She speaks from the Episcopal polity perspective, but I believe her recommendations have universal applicability and can help a congregation avoid the worst of the systemic impact of misconduct through healthy practices of transparency and listening.

The question often remains, however, how congregations who experienced misconduct in their *past* should surface and talk about it in the *present*. For some people, it will be "old news" that they would rather not dwell on. People newer to the congregation will struggle to find its relevance. Nevertheless, there are still healthy practices that can be followed by acknowledging past misconduct and its impact on the system. One need not reveal the whole story, chapter and verse, to be able to say: "we experienced this kind of misconduct and it impacted us this way." Often, the most powerful testimonials can come from those who are willing to talk about how they experienced the misconduct (with necessary cautions against placing abuse survivors in this position). Just this level of transparency can introduce air into the system and allow the toxicity of secrecy to disperse.

Again, as stated above, misconduct does not have to be sexual to still have lasting and damaging impact on a congregation. Emotional manipulation can happen at all levels. My denomination has only recently started to confront the detrimental effects of a minister who bullies or mistreats staff, and to remove such ministers from fellowship. This behavior has impact far beyond the staff affected, as the congregation begins to mistrust and misunderstand the staff. Simmering tensions can be picked up subliminally, and rising systemic anxiety results.

Confronting misconduct is some of the hardest work a congregation can do. No one would choose to do so if they didn't have to. But, when good processes are followed and transparency is assured, a congregation can often emerge stronger than ever before.

Questions for Discussion

- Has there been a history of misconduct in your congregation? How was it processed?
- Does it seem that there are "secrets" about the past that are felt but not acknowledged?
- What would your personal response be if your minister engaged in misconduct?

Chapter Seven

Conflicts about Race

Do not be daunted by the enormity of the world's grief. Do justly now, love mercy now, walk humbly now. You are not obligated to complete the work, but neither are you free to abandon it.

—The Talmud, *Interpretive translation of Talmudic texts*

My call to ministry was intimately tied up with a call to justice. I originally tried to work out that call in electoral politics, and ultimately found that arena to be empty of the soul work required to do justice. Ministry felt like the way I could engage with people's minds, hearts, and souls to go deeper than changing laws or policies ever could. This call also led me to pursue ministries with congregations that had some diversity in its constituents, believing that therein the beloved community lay.

And my first two ministries were indeed with two of the more racially diverse congregations in my denomination, in Detroit and in Chicago. For a girl from a small town in Texas, simply living in those cities was an education in and of itself. The deeply rooted systemic racism that resulted in the near destruction of the city of Detroit was evident to me every day. The congregation I served was one of the few mostly White congregations that stayed downtown when most had fled to the suburbs. That the congregation was roughly 30 percent Black was a source of pride (to the White folks at least). I learned of the fortitude it required of Black people to be in the midst of Whiteness. A Black woman who had been a member of the church for 30 years once said to me: "Whenever the White folks get crazy, I just go upstairs and volunteer in the church school. There's much more sanity to be found with children." In Detroit I worked hard to develop relationships with community organizations and justice groups and Black churches. I believe I prided myself on this work to the point where it felt like I "got it"—I understood the nature of racial dynamics and thought I was poised to help bring about change. The congregation had relatively few overt skirmishes over issues of race, so I hadn't had to confront the fallacy of my pride.

The second church I served in Chicago was another story. This was the time when Unitarian Universalist congregations were trying to grapple with internal homophobia through the previously referenced program, "The Welcoming Congregation." It was important and difficult work, and it exposed long-simmering frustrations and divisions among the people of color in the church. "Why are we suddenly so concerned with welcoming gay people when we still don't really know how to welcome Black people?" was a refrain I often heard. Let me be clear, I have sometimes heard people assert that Black people are more homophobic than White people. *I do not believe that.* For a people who have been repeatedly punished, in the most dire fashion, for any kind of sexual expression, it becomes a more complicated subject.

I had hired a staff person who was Black and queer, and initially she and I enjoyed a dynamic working relationship. While I knew I had a lot to learn from her, again I felt the hubris of feeling like I had "arrived" at a great understanding of Black people. As we went through the Welcoming Congregation process it became clear to her, at least, that I really didn't fully get it. The complexity of being a queer Black person in this context left her feeling pulled in a multitude of directions, and I often expected her to be the "emissary" to the Black people. She began to feel less and less understood and supported by me. I began to feel more and more betrayed by her. Didn't she understand what I had done for her? You can imagine how this goes from here.

This, and several other painful experiences I had with Black people in that setting, began to make it apparent to me that I still had learning to do, but the pain of those experiences overwhelmed my desire to learn, and I shut down. While I continued to do some racial justice work, internally I felt cynical, bitter, and hopeless. Internally, I walked away from the work. Because, as a White person, I could.

Essentially, I was fearful of examining my own racial reckoning. I didn't know if I had the fortitude to do it. It wasn't until the murder of

Michael Brown, in Ferguson, Missouri, that I began to stir out of my own self-absorbed resistance and start to engage more fully again. Participating in the Black Lives Matter movement brought my soul alive again for racial justice work. Ironically, it feels even more daunting now than it ever has before, but I feel gripped by its necessity and can't release that grip.

I tell this story at some length to show that I understand how difficult the work of racial justice can be. Congregations across the country have had to be rudely awakened to the need to do this work, and some have been paralyzed by it. Even in all-White congregations, the conflict has arisen in more profound ways than ever before. I know of Black congregations with rifts as well, as they confront the different worldviews that are held by younger people active in the movement. Those schooled in the art of "respectability politics" have had their assumptions rocked by the confrontative strategies of younger activists.

I want to be clear, here, that I speak only from the experience of leading mostly White congregations. The examples I will offer as case studies are of mostly White congregations who have struggled with conflicts about race. I would be interested to learn how mostly Black congregations work through their conflicts, but that is beyond my experience. I wish I could say that these stories all resulted in great, transformative change. Those that didn't can still offer us learnings as we examine them. And I hope some of them will inspire you and give you courage to engage with issues that may have previously seemed frightening and impossible to name.

Harriet was the White minister of a growing mid-sized church in the suburbs beyond a mostly Black city. The congregation had a few people of color, but it was very active in community social justice and racial justice activities. The church was growing beyond the capacity of their building, so the leadership went out to explore possibilities. They came upon a downtown church that was selling their building due to their dwindling congregation. The building was large enough to allow Harriet's church to grow, and so the congregation voted to buy and restore it. They began to create trusted relationships in the neighborhood, and their social justice ministries were mushrooming. They held services both downtown and in their suburban building, but the hope was to ultimately completely move downtown.

Before that could take place, however, an economic downturn hit the city and the crime rate skyrocketed. A murder happened just outside the door of the church during services, which rocked many people's sense of safety. It was becoming clear that there were a number of people in the congregation who simply hadn't been present for the vote to buy the building, and they were now agitating to return completely to the suburban church. Harriet and much of the leadership had thought that the holdouts would eventually just come along, but instead they gained traction through activating people's fears. They began to reduce the services downtown to only once a month. It became apparent that there wasn't the support to continue to maintain the downtown ministry, and Harriet left the church in dejection.

This is a story that could be told as an example of the futility of getting a White congregation to really engage in deep social and racial justice work. But there are some learnings that can be gleaned. It makes clear that the excitement that can surround a new venture cannot be sustained when the inevitable failures occur along the way, without deeper work to undergird the change. I wonder if it would have been possible to build a broader consensus around the decision, by taking the time to really engage almost *everyone* in how this move could help them better fulfill their mission.

This story took place before the Black Lives Matter movement helped make it clear to many mostly White congregations that there is deep work for us to do to confront the White supremacy systems in our midst. This is not about doing something for the community *out there.* It requires internal examination on a personal and systemic level. If it had been possible to undertake work of this depth as the congregation was making this decision, it may not have been possible for people to hide behind fears of "crime" and instead help them uncover what it really means to put themselves into a Black context.

Another story takes place while Black Lives Matter was first exploding on the scene. Jennifer was serving as an interim minister in a congregation in a diverse Southern city that also had some level of diversity itself. In the past there had not been many blow-ups about race. The church had had a troubled history in general, including a minister who had committed suicide, and a building that was flooded beyond repair. Finding resilience in the face of these adversities was the first order of business for this interim time. And the congregation began to find this strength, successfully raising the money for and ultimately erecting a beautiful new building. But as the country began to confront racism in a new way, the congregation began to have to do so as well.

A prominent Black lay person who had been active in the congregation for some time began to voice her adamant frustration with what she perceived as the congregation's resistance to the work of racial justice. The older White liberal members took affront as they had been at the forefront of school desegregation battles and thought that "proved" that they weren't racist, which was how they heard her protests. Older Black members who had mostly settled into the White context by believing they needed to be "nice," thought this lay person's tactics of confrontation were counterproductive. Younger Black folks were stepping right up into the agitation, and middle-aged White folks who felt that their conservatism shouldn't be confronted dug in. Outraged letters started to fly, and sides were being taken.

Jennifer, the interim minister, tried to defuse the situation with some humor. "Can we all just agree that we can make this conflict much worse? Let's take this out of the parking lot and just start talking to one another." Conflict coaches were engaged and conversation tools were tried. The polarization eased, but the ever-evolving drama of racism in America kept reigniting the flames. Making "defunding the police" the rallying cry when the chief of police was in the congregation did not go over well! Eventually they did find a framework that is now helping the congregation have the deeper conversations—a denominational initiative which frames the need to confront White supremacy as a core principle. Jennifer encouraged them to believe that they could tell a new story about themselves as a congregation, one that has multiple levels of resilience and strength. They have since called a new Black minister to serve them. All involved know this will be an uphill challenge, but they feel they have laid the groundwork for the complex conversations that will help get them through.

DEAR WHITE PEOPLE

Just as I specifically addressed clergy in chapter 3, here I want to address White people. I can't speak for people of color and I can't suggest anything for people of color to do, as that is their prerogative. But I can say to White people: it is time for us to listen.

When I plumb my own story for lessons learned, the major one that jumps out at me is that I needed to listen more. Back to our core principles of conflict transformation: I made too many assumptions, about myself and others, and I didn't listen well. Liberal White people are often so anxious to prove their anti-racist bona fides that we talk before we listen. Again, remember what we have learned about anxiety: it shuts down our ability to understand complexity. Numerous books have addressed what we, as White people, need to learn.[1] But for the purposes of this book, I want to return again to the wisdom of Resmaa Menakem.

Menakem's caution that we cannot cure racism with our heads, requires us to return to what we now understand about our bodies' response to conflict. He specifically addresses white people here:

> White-body supremacy also harms people who do not have dark skin. If you're a white American, your body has probably inherited a different legacy of trauma that affects white bodies—and, at times, may rekindle old flight, flee, or freeze responses. This trauma goes back centuries—at least as far back as the Middle Ages—and has been passed down from one white body to another for dozens of generations.[2]

This is not to say that White people are allowed to play victim, but that we need to acknowledge that racial trauma has affected our bodies as well, even if differently than the bodies of culture, as Menakem names them. If we pass by our own trauma, whistling our anxiety into the wind, we will never get to the point of helping to heal what I believe to be the greatest disease in our nation. Addressing that trauma requires us to work with our bodies in all the ways we have been talking about in this book.

It takes continuous discipline to remind ourselves over and over to listen—to listen to others, as well as to listen to our own bodies. Menakem reminds us of this:

> In today's America, we tend to think of healing as something binary: either we're broken or we're healed from that brokenness. But that's not how healing operates, and it's almost never how human growth works. More often, healing and growth take place on a continuum, with innumerable points between utter brokenness and total health.[3]

Just as our work with conflict, in general, is a journey, our work with racial conflict is a journey. It is one that we can make progress on, if we can begin with listening.

TRUTH AND RECONCILIATION

Sometimes a congregation grapples with the difficult truth of recognizing its own complicity in racial injustice in its history, leading to necessary work in the present. This can be a painful and conflict-ridden process, but also one that presents the greatest potential for transformation that I've seen.

Numerous congregations and institutions have been taking difficult but unflinching looks at their basis in a slaveholding past, and creating processes of restitution. One congregation's story stands out for me. (Unlike other stories told in this book, this one is not altered for privacy.) The Memorial Episcopal Church in Baltimore's Bolton Hill is a largely White, socially liberal congregation of moderate size. When the Reverend Grey Maggiano arrived as a new rector at Memorial in 2017, he was attracted by its reputation for progressive social justice work. But he began to wonder why, with all its activism, it was still a mostly White congregation in the midst of a mostly Black neighborhood. Maggiano began to delve into the congregation's past, and realized that in fact, Memorial

was for generations a bastion of racial segregation. Nineteenth-century property records showed that Howard, members of his extended family, and many of the parish's early worshipers were slave owners and Confederate sympathizers.

Segregationism became part of its identity. Marble plaques that flank the entrance commemorate Howard, who Maggiano says saw it as his duty to serve as a ballast against social change, and Henry Van Dyke Johns, the rector of Emmanuel Episcopal Church in Mount Vernon, a cleric who enjoyed widespread respect but also owned slaves.

After Johns died in 1859, Memorial was established to honor his memory.[4]

In the decades following, church leaders supported segregation and "protective" neighborhood societies, held minstrel shows, and berated parishioners who belonged to organizations such as the National

Association for the Advancement of Colored People (NAACP). They did not admit black members until 1969.

Rather than leaping into "solving" this problem, the church began a process of deep examination both internally and externally, and developed relationships with neighborhood African American congregations and organizations. On a more deeply personal level, a Black deacon, the Reverend Natalie Conway, discovered that her ancestors were slaves on the plantation owned by the founding pastor, Charles Ridgely Howard, and a Howard descendant, Steve Howard, was a current and active parishioner. The shock of these personal connections led Conway to educate herself and the congregation about this history, and she and Howard worked together to lead the congregation in liturgical ceremonies of reconciliation. From Steve Howard's perspective, he

> had always known of his ancestors' slave owning past, but "kept it at an intellectual level" until Conway's story emerged. He's still grappling with its implications, but says addressing their joint history—though it felt like a "punch in the gut"—was important.
> "This has been a giant step forward," he said.[5]

All of this internal work has resulted in the church promising to dedicate $500,000 over the next five years by establishing a reparations fund. They will donate to and support local community organizations doing "justice-centered work."[6]

It is hard to imagine that this process was easy for all concerned. In fact, Conway considered ending the relationship. She says, "My initial reaction was, 'Why should I stay at a place that enslaved my ancestors? . . . I need to leave this church."[7] "Instead, she has helped lead her congregation on a journey."[8] Painful as it has been on all sides, the congregation has truly transformed through this effort. A 15-year-old parishioner, Daviedra Saulsberry, who is Black, reflects on the process she has been witnessing in her church: "as hard as it is to watch Conway and Howard air truths that might have been left unspoken, the struggles are leading to growth for everyone taking part. 'It has been remarkable to see reconciliation taking place literally before my eyes.'"[9]

Many other congregations are undergoing other forms of Truth and Reconciliation work. Some, like the congregation I currently serve, are grappling with the fact that prominent lay people and ministers in their past have actively supported and promoted eugenics. Others are wrestling with their denomination's legacies of participating in the near-extinction of Native American peoples and cultures. The horrifying stories that have emerged recently of unnamed bodies being unearthed on the grounds of religious schools bring this collusion to light.

Engaging in work such as this shows that the issues involved are not just social or political. They can, in fact, be deeply theological. In the instance of Unitarian Universalism, one need only probe into the interpretation of humanist thought that encourages the idea that we can control and try to perfect all of human experience. For Christian churches, many are grappling with the "Christian exceptionalism" that undergirds the disregard, and ultimate dismantlement, of other cultures and traditions. While this may seem daunting and discouraging, many are finding an unexpected feeling of liberation. One colleague put it this way: "It can be horrifying to think that my religious ancestors whom I used to admire and exalt behaved in ways I now find unforgiveable. But then I realize that by looking more deeply at their stories and this history, I can begin to question how I might be falling under the spell of the same fallacies. And that, ultimately, is worth the effort." Pain faced can be pain redeemed.

Questions for Discussion

- In what ways have conflicts about race been manifest in your congregation?
- How do these conflicts make you feel?
- What have been your methods for addressing them (both individually and within your congregation?)
- How might you approach them going forward?

Part II

STRATEGIES FOR CHANGE

Chapter Eight

Creating a New Culture of Learning

A spirit of exploration requires both a firm conviction about the purpose and destination of the expedition and an equal awareness of what is not known about the territory to be explored. "Ignoramus," from the Latin, means "we do not know." Ignorance, in the sense of ignoramus, has become pejoratively connected with stupidity, a lack of good judgment—not a good place from which to lead. However, the healthier understanding of ignorance suggests that it is the source of inquiry—the place from which all learning begins because "we do not know." It is a significant part of the substantive work of new leadership to protect ignorance, to eschew flimsy certainty, to avoid casting partial answers as if they are final solutions, and to insist on the hard work of learning.

—Gil Rendle[1]

Congregations can easily get stuck in ruts of doing the same thing over and over again. There are many deep psychological reasons why we avoid trying something new or admitting that we may not have all the answers. However, as we've been discussing throughout this book, the challenges we now face require us to do just that, in spite of the discomfort. Not only do the crises of the times ask us to learn new ways, our spirits actually call out for it, even if that call is quelled by anxiety at times. Again, Gil Rendle describes:

When problem solving is the dominant agenda, energy and hope leave the room. Given . . . that so much of what faces leaders is, in fact, not a

95

"problem" because the deep changes faced are without "solution," the futility of solving problems in order to return to a time that no longer exists exhausts and depletes leaders. Sitting in yet one more problem-solving group deflates leaders. However, remembering and staying connected to purpose energizes leaders, and subsequently hope grows. With hope, and with the companionship and challenge of other purposeful colleagues, courage grows.[2]

If we can quiet the anxious amygdala that calls out for easy solutions, we can begin to find the energy to explore something new.

BUILDING CONGREGATIONAL CAPACITY

Ultimately what we are trying to build is the congregation's capacity to grow and learn over time. That means developing:

- The capacity to see (to pay attention to) what is really in front of us and what we are really doing.
- The capacity to integrate, to bring pieces together to help the whole make sense.
- The capacity to engage dilemmas, to not shy away from the challenging questions.
- The capacity to make complexity a friend, allowing multiple versions of truth to coexist with one another.
- And, the capacity to hear and engage multiple voices, to find ways to include the whole congregation and its many parts.

ADAPTIVE LEADERSHIP

It will be helpful at this point to introduce a theory of leadership that has been hugely influential in developing my understanding of change in congregations. Many are probably already familiar with it. Ron Heifetz of the Harvard Business School is the creative genius behind this theory of Adaptive Leadership, and many of his practitioners and colleagues have taken it even further.[3] Exploring its many complexities would take us beyond the scope of this book, but some core concepts are very relevant for our work.

To begin, Adaptive Leadership makes a distinction between technical problems and adaptive challenges. Technical problems are things that can be fixed by bringing the right expertise to bear. This doesn't mean that they are simple, as there are incredibly complex technical problems. But they can be resolved and, when they are, order is restored. Think of that old organ that keeps breaking down. It may be hard these days to find a technician who understands tracker organs, but once you've found one, you can be good to go the next Sunday!

Adaptive challenges, on the other hand, are those issues that are not necessarily resolvable. You may not even know what the right question is, let alone the answer. It may be easy to technically fix the organ's pipes once you find the right person, but other questions inevitably arise. "Where will the money come from?" "If it will cost $200,000 to fix, is that the best use of our funds?" "Do younger generations appreciate the organ?" "Shouldn't we spend our money on religious education, or social justice?" You can see these questions spiraling into conflicts almost immediately! As much as we might like to think there's a perfect fundraising plan out there that can solve this problem, it should already be apparent that these issues run deeper than that. They make us question our core values, such as: Who are we trying to reach with our worship services? They create confusion and disequilibrium: Who gets to make these decisions? As Rendle notes, leaders need to embrace ignorance in the best sense of the word: "It is a significant part of the substantive work of new leadership to protect ignorance, to eschew flimsy certainty, to avoid casting partial answers as if they are final solutions, and to insist on the hard work of learning."[4]

These are challenges that can't be solved. Progress on them can be made, but the traditional idea of getting the right kind of leader to bring order to the chaos won't work here. In fact, Heifetz questions many of our assumptions about leadership in general. Whereas typically we have understood leadership as something that resides in particular kinds of people with particular kinds of personalities, Heifetz talks about leadership as a *verb*—the act of mobilizing people to take on the tough challenges. This is work anyone can do, not just those who are typically thought of as leaders. The work of Adaptive Leadership is all about adaptation and experimentation. It requires perspective on both the past and the potential future. This kind of leadership doesn't solve conflicts—it often generates them! No one is expert enough to be the leader who finds the solution.

Relevant to the question of how we grow congregational capacity, Adaptive Leadership encourages the skill of getting up on the balcony. As Heifetz and colleagues explain:

> To diagnose a system or yourself while in the midst of action requires the ability to achieve some distance from those on-the-ground events. We use the metaphor of "getting on the balcony" above the "dance floor" to depict what it means to gain the distanced perspective you need to see what is really happening. If you stay on the dance floor, all you will see will be the people dancing with you and around you. Swept up in the music, it may be a great party! But when you get on the balcony, you may see a very different picture. From that vantage point, you might notice that the band is playing so loudly that everyone is dancing on the far side of the room, that when the music changes from fast to slow (or back again), different groups of people decide to dance, and that many people hang back near the exit doors and do not dance, whatever the music. Not such a great party after all. If someone asked you to later describe the dance, you would paint a very different picture if you had seen it from the balcony rather than only from the dance floor.[5]

A mid-size church had been struggling with its religious education program. It had the practice of sending the children out to their classes after a few minutes in the worship service—the assumption being that children find it difficult to sit still in worship and that they may not be interested in what the adults were interested in. This practice had the effect of making it difficult to recruit teachers, because the adults wanted to stay in the service. Heidi, the minister, decided to flip the question: What if we made worship interesting for all ages? They began to poll potential teachers to see if they would be willing to stay after the service to teach, and the response was overwhelmingly, yes. Heidi began to pay more attention to how worship could appeal to all ages, and the young people actually stayed! In particular it was appealing to the teenage youth in the congregation who had been spending most of their time at church in their own little room, but who now could understand the bigger picture of what worship was all about. Heidi managed to get them onto the balcony to look at a different experience of the dance floor.

Another key concept of Adaptive Leadership that is relevant to what we have been exploring—*productive disequilibrium:*

To practice adaptive leadership, you have to help people navigate through a period of disturbance as they sift through what is essential and what is expendable. . . . This disequilibrium can catalyze everything from conflict, frustration, and panic, to confusion, disorientation, and fear of losing something dear. That is not what you are paid to do and will certainly not be as well received as when you are mobilizing people to address a technical issue. . . . Consequently, when you are practicing adaptive leadership, distinctive skills and insights are necessary to deal with this swirling mass of energies. You need to be able to do two things: (1) manage yourself in that environment and (2) help people tolerate the discomfort that they are experiencing. You need to live into the disequilibrium.[6]

Remember Irene's church that I talked about in chapter 5? What the congregation clearly learned from their experience with the antagonistic president, was that they could not keep brushing conflicts under the rug. They took themselves through a rigorous process of learning how to work *with* conflict. They established a healthy congregation team separate from leadership that could help train the congregation, as well as mediate disputes. They utilized a worksheet that another congregation developed for people to fill out when they thought they were in conflict. It asks all the self-reflective questions that I have been promoting! Questions such as "What is your relationship to the people involved?" "What are your feelings?" "In what way does the conflict affect you?" I have put the entire form as an appendix to this book. The congregation found that by asking people to engage in this self-reflection at the beginning of the process, the level of anxiety was reduced to the point that they could have a more complex conversation about the issues. In essence, they created a method to ensure productive disequilibrium!

You can see how the skills of conflict transformation that I have been exploring are necessary for this kind of work. When people are overwhelmed by disequilibrium, they will not be able to productively contribute (remember the amygdala!). But if your response is to try to eliminate the disequilibrium, you will never be able to motivate people to make the changes that are necessary to address the challenge.

When I have introduced Adaptive Leadership practices to congregations, I often hear something akin to "But we don't want to do it that way!" Just as our culture doesn't prepare us with healthy conflict skills, we are mostly rewarded for our technical expertise. The problem, of course, is that we don't usually have a choice. You can fling all the technical solutions you want at an adaptive challenge and they will never really solve your problem. Finding ways to hold yourself in a learning mode, calming anxiety through the methods we have been learning, will ultimately unleash the creativity Gil Rendle describes above. It just takes going through some hard places to get there.

THE ART OF POWERFUL QUESTIONS

If part of the work of Adaptive Leadership is not assuming you know what the question is, then it can be helpful to think about our very practice of asking questions. Think of these examples:

- What will it take to fix the organ?
- How might we think about the organ repair in the context of exploring how we live out our mission?

Which question do you think will help create the most productive and creative conversation?

Sometimes it is so wonderful to come across a resource that you can read in one sitting! In 16 short pages, Eric Vogt and colleagues wrote "The Art and Architecture of Powerful Questions," which is an amazing resource for setting up conversations that will open things up rather than shut them down. In their definition, a powerful question:

- Stimulates reflective thinking
- Challenges assumptions
- Is thought-provoking
- Generates energy and a vector to explore
- Channels inquiry, promises insight
- Is broad and enduring
- Touches a deeper meaning
- Evokes more questions.[7]

Sounds easy, right? Not necessarily. Again, it is an underdeveloped skill in our culture, which has a decided preference for questions that have obvious answers. But if I had to choose just one tool in a leadership body's tool kit, it would be this one. Asking people yes or no questions invites polarization. Asking questions that already have a lot of assumptions buried in them implies a not-so-hidden agenda. But a truly powerful question can take you, and the congregation, to places you may not have been able to imagine. It takes practice, but it is worth it.

As we have already explored, surfacing our own assumptions can be a tricky thing to do. We need partners in this work, which is why this is such a great exercise for leadership bodies. When I first learned this technique, the instructor had us present our powerful question to the rest of the students. She had given us all placards numbered 1 through 5; 1 indicates the most powerful question, and 5, the least. The group then "voted" on the questions each of us developed. When I looked at the 3s, 4s and even 5s my questions were judged, it was rather a rude awakening for me to realize I didn't know how to do this very well! "Did you realize that you're assuming A in that question?" and "Don't you think that B will lead to a yes or no response?" were typical comments. But the process helped! We learned some of the best ways to start a question: for example, to begin with *how might we*, was far more powerful than *who*, *when*, or *what*, which call for a concrete response. Vogt tends to promote *why* as a good start, but I have learned to question that practice. My experience is that asking *why* can make it sound like an interrogation. Working the question as a leadership group can help refine your thinking and better understand your goals, and eliminate hidden assumptions. Giving small groups the most powerful question to dwell on can dictate the success, or lack thereof, of the conversation.

In a workshop I conducted recently, I was trying to give people the experience of how small-group conversations could open up a dialogue. I asked them to give me an example of a big question they were struggling with, and they came up with: "How can we grow the congregation?" I assume that you can probably spot the assumptions in that question! We were in a bit of a hurry so I didn't stop to help refine the question. When we started the small group, "Why do we think we need to grow, aren't we good enough the way we are?" was the beginning salvo, and it went downhill from there. If the question had been something like: "How can we have the greatest impact on the lives of our members and our surrounding community?" that might have gotten us further. Powerful questions are the ones that help us relax into the dialogue and feel empowered to explore. Not-so-powerful questions just create polarization and resistance.

THE POWER OF A POSITIVE NO

I introduced this tool in chapter 3 when discussing self-understanding. It can also be a helpful tool for organizations as well. Congregational leaders can be terribly reluctant to confront difficult issues, particularly related to staff concerns. But by focusing on what you are trying to say "yes" to—healthy staff culture, for example—it can be a bit easier to say "no" to someone who is destructive to the system.

A church that was well-known for its wonderful music program was in a quandary: the famed music director who had created this fabulous program was, frankly, a nightmare to work with. She undermined staff and lay leadership alike, assuming her prominent public reputation would make her untouchable. A consultant came to help the board discern possible ways of dealing with this challenge. The first thing the consultant did was to have each board member describe their experience of working with the music director. As they went around the table there grew a palpable sense of relief. Each person thought they were alone in having difficulties with this staff member. Once it became clear that there was an obvious need to address the problem, the consultant helped them work through their fear of letting go of this popular director. "What are you saying yes to, when you say the director has to go?" They generated a list of positive dynamics they were trying to create in the church culture. Out of that they were able to craft a communication to the congregation to help explain why they had to let the music director go. There was a reaction, but it passed fairly quickly once people understood and began to experience the positive changes that occurred.

TAKING TIME

There is Enough Time. Wherever we practice, time is the most common resource that feels scarce. Time is one of our greatest common practice areas of scarcity. Let people know there is enough time for them, for their feelings and needs to be met, for their future to be shaped.[8]

This wisdom from adrienne maree brown is absolutely key for transformational processes. If I had to name the number-one mistake that congregations make in working through conflicts, it would be that they rushed them through. And why would we want to rush? Anxiety, of course! It is also one of the named elements of White supremacy culture: "a continued sense of urgency that makes it difficult to take time to be inclusive, encourage democratic and/or thoughtful decision-making, to think long-term, to consider consequences."[9]

Unless your congregation is about to freeze or burn down, there is always more time to work through a challenging conflict. All of these processes and practices that I describe in this chapter and the next require time that will at some point make some people frustrated and anxious. Note the mistake I made above in my workshop that didn't take time to fully craft a powerful question. The anxiety that gets revealed when things get rushed is a signal that you should slow things down. When I am coaching people in effective preaching or public speaking, I always say to them: "If you think you are going too slowly, slow down!" Anxiety in public speaking makes you speed up, which compromises your message. The same is true with adaptive challenges. It will always go more slowly than you think it should, and that is a good thing.

A fast-growing congregation was confronting the fact that their growth didn't always make for a great experience for all. The sanctuary was bursting every Sunday, which, ironically, made people feel less welcome because there wasn't room for them. At the social hour after service, the room was so crowded that a person could hardly move from one spot in the room to another. The congregation was a tight community; people enjoyed seeing everyone they knew during the service. When it was proposed that they move to two services, it was not a popular idea. People worried that it would split the community, and they would miss seeing everyone at one service. The decision was finally made to make the transition to two services, with one major codicil: the decision would be actively revisited at every annual meeting for the next three years. That helped make it palatable for those who didn't like the idea. Church members felt like they would be empowered to question the change on a regular basis. Once they started the new practice, people began to realize that it was not only possible to see old friends, but they could also make new ones!

Taking time helps bring along those who may be resisting a change. But it also helps you make a *better decision*, because you have taken time to explore all the possibilities.

MISTAKES: AN ESSENTIAL PART OF LEARNING

As we discover in childhood, learning is not always an easy process. Those first spills we take when we are learning to walk are actually important ways for the body to learn balance. Probably not a comfort for a father anxiously watching as his child lands on her face, but important learning nonetheless.

The same is certainly true in establishing a culture of learning in a congregation. It is not always an excitingly creative and engaging enterprise! We inevitably will make mistakes along the way, the more so if we allow ourselves to flex the muscle of engaging in experiments. Mistakes are hard for many to acknowledge, however. There is an unfortunate association of mistakes with failure. This goes against the grain with our often-perfectionistic cultures. Perfectionism is yet another aspect of White supremacy culture named by Jones and Okun that needs to be evaluated. The challenges of perfectionism are named here:

- little appreciation expressed among people for the work that others are doing—appreciation that is expressed usually directed to those who get most of the credit anyway;
- more common is to point out either how the person or work is inadequate;
- or even more common, to talk to others about the inadequacies of a person or their work without ever talking directly to them;
- mistakes are seen as personal, i.e. they reflect badly on the person making them as opposed to being seen for what they are—mistakes;
- making a mistake is confused with being a mistake, doing wrong with being wrong;
- little time, energy, or money put into reflection or identifying lessons learned that can improve practice, in other words little or no learning from mistakes; and
- tendency to identify what is wrong; little ability to identify, name, and appreciate what is right.[10]

Is this starting to sound familiar? In order for a culture to begin to shift toward a healthy naming of, and learning from, mistakes, the leadership must model the behavior.

A New England congregation known for its soaring and beautiful steeple was approached by a cell phone company that was searching for places to situate their cell phone towers without marring the charming New England landscape. Positioning it in a steeple where no one would see it seemed a logical choice. They were prepared to pay generously, not just for the construction of the tower, but also ongoing maintenance of the steeple. The minister of this congregation was out of the country on sabbatical, so the board had to deal with this decision themselves. Given that they had been recently grappling with how they were going to pay for much-needed repairs to the steeple, this seemed like an easy decision! The company was pressing for a quick response (remember the caution about time!), and so they voted as a board to accept the proposal. They presented it to the congregation as the answer to their prayers!

The congregation, however, did not see it that way. Immediately there was a firestorm of concerns: What were the potential health risks of a cell tower? Did the church want to be beholden to a corporation, of all things? And more. The board, taken aback by this unexpected criticism, started to feel defensive and doubled down on their decision. The congregation members felt pressured to choose a side, and polarization soared. A congregational meeting was called for, and they were about to hold one, when a respected elder on the board declared: "We are not going to hold a vote. We should use this experience to learn how to create transparency and give opportunities for congregational feedback. No amount of money is worth splitting the church over." The rest of the board immediately recognized and endorsed this wisdom.

It is one thing for lay leadership to admit to mistakes. It is another thing altogether for ministers to do so. We often feel the pressure to be completely confident in whatever decision we make. As Jenny Smith, the pastor and writer whom I referenced in chapter 3, put it this way:

> The last few generations have valued professionalism over honesty. Politeness over authenticity. Strength over weakness. As the tides change and new generations lift up shifting values, many of us are caught in the middle. Our hearts long to be honest, authentic and explore our weakness. We know deeper strength lies in that intersection.
> But the air we breathe tells a different story. *Suck it up.*
> Keep that to yourself.
> Do your job.

Keep it together.

We don't talk about that here.

So we claw our way back onto our pedestal, as if we can ward off the dissonance between our heart and the expectations in the air. We continue the cruel game that requires a pastor to live on a pedestal for all to see. It slowly turns as a human somehow becomes an example of how to live, how to be peaceful, how to be good.[11]

Particularly when we are in a period of great cultural consternation, as we are at this moment in the pandemic, we feel obliged to be a model of certainty and calm. But one of the most powerful tools in a minister's arsenal is the power of confession. The story below shows an example of this.

Martha and Steven were called as co-ministers to a congregation with the stated intention by the search committee that they bring strong administrative skills. (Search committees are often out ahead of their congregations. When ministers complain to me that the search committee told them that X is the highest priority and that doing X got them into terrible trouble, my response is often, "And you believed them?!") When they started making good on what they thought was a clear expectation, they encountered massive resistance from the chair and vice-chair of their board, who experienced their actions as grabbing the power away from lay leadership. Explanations of streamlining decision-making, and empowering ministers to do their jobs, fell on deaf ears and, in some ways, fanned the flames. This conflict eventually spilled out into the open with the two board folks publicly denigrating Steven and Martha.

The ministers were full of their own righteousness about how they were just doing what they thought they were called to do, but, again, a wise elder asked them to rethink their approach and their actions. Eventually they began to process for themselves some mistakes that they had made along the way in how they had ignored signals of discomfort, and left legitimate concerns unaddressed. The board finally called for an open congregational meeting (you know what I think of those!). But the ministers completely defused the conflict by openly acknowledging and naming the mistakes they had made. It took another year and a half to get their ministry back on track, but that confessional moment turned the tide in a healthy direction.

As I said earlier, learning is not always easy! And keeping a congregational culture open to learning, even when mistakes are made and anxiety spikes, is even more difficult. But it leads the way to a far healthier congregation.

Helene was serving a large congregation that prided itself on its vitality. Helene was not completely beloved by the congregation, but most were content with her ministry. When she decided to retire, the leadership thought that this was an opportunity to bring in a more dynamic young minister. They had been told by several church consultants that they were extremely healthy and that there should be no reason that they could not go straight into a new ministry without an interim period.

The search committee for the next minister then felt like they had to work quickly to find the new minister the congregation seemed to want. They interviewed Pasqual, who certainly seemed to bring the charisma they were looking for. But Pasqual was a newly minted minister without a lot of experience in a large church. The committee was torn about recommending him, but finally thought that the congregation was healthy enough to nurture a young leader. And they dreaded the idea of going back to the congregation without a clear choice.

Pasqual began with great excitement on all sides. But very quickly it became clear that he didn't really understand administration in a complex system. A number of lay leaders tried to coach him through learning about budgeting and financial management, but he was often too embarrassed to admit that he needed help. He hired a bookkeeper who was not much more experienced, and together they failed to pay thousands of dollars of retirement funds for the rest of the staff. By the time the mistake was discovered, the church was over $100,000 in arrears. Again, Pasqual found it difficult to admit he needed help, so the leadership felt they had no choice but to let him go.

The leadership began to recognize the ways in which the precipitousness of their search process had contributed to the position they were in. The implicit assumption that a search committee would fail if they did not bring forward a candidate was clearly counterproductive. Leaders also began to admit that perhaps the congregation was not necessarily the beacon of health that they had assumed themselves to be. The church went into a deliberate interim process with full acknowledgment of previous mistakes and with a determination to learn new lessons, even if they were difficult ones. The next called minister was certainly dynamic, but she also brought with her some significant management experience that was much needed. Mistakes would still be made on all parts! But taking a humble posture and recognizing the learning that needed to take place put the congregation on a healthy new path.

In the next chapter I will introduce some more specific tools that will help hold a congregation in a learning mode, as well as to walk through challenging conflicts. It can be done!

Questions for Discussion

- What are ways in which we have named learning goals for congregation?
- Are there times when our congregation has been engaging in perfectionistic thinking? Are there mistakes from our past that we can acknowledge and learn from?
- Have there been examples of ways in which we have mistaken adaptive challenges for technical ones, and then tried to "fix them?"
- Have we made some decisions perhaps too precipitously?
- What would you say are the three most important things your congregation needs to engage in learning about?

Chapter Nine

Tools for Change

As a society, we are convinced that if we can only learn enough, become strong enough, and work hard enough, we can impose peace and fulfillment upon ourselves and everyone else. But the actual condition of the world and of our own hearts refutes this. Something else is needed: some source of inspiration, some reservoir of power and wisdom beyond that which is provided by our personal wills. We need something that can balance willfulness with willingness, something that can temper our harshness with love.[11]

—Gerald May

Now that we understand more about the dynamics of conflict, we can start to explore concrete tools that can assist us in addressing conflicts in congregations. Each of them requires us to practice adaptive leadership, or, in Gerald May's terms, to balance willfulness with willingness, to temper . . . with love (Ibid). My presentation of these is not meant to be sequential. At the end of this chapter I'll talk about how they may be put together. But for now I'll just share with you some of the methods I have used that have been helpful.

COVENANTS

Many congregations try to establish covenants of right relations in order to set some guidelines about healthy behavior. And indeed, it is far more helpful to let people know in advance about what to avoid rather than trying to explain why it was problematic in the moment. As we learned in Irene's story, naming and educating a congregation about what makes for *good* behavior helps mitigate against the *bad* behavior. In my denomination we started using this tool with deliberation in the 1980s, and it has been used ever since with mostly great effect.

Particularly in my tradition, which is covenantal rather than creedal, it behooves us to express, in concrete terms as well as theological terms, what it means to make covenant our organizing principle. In a recent report from the UUA Commission on Appraisal (an elected body that convenes every few years to examine important issues within Unitarian Universalism) the theory and practice of covenants was explored:

> *We* are a covenantal faith. We promise each other to behave in certain ways and create common aspirations. We set our lives around the praxis of living out the promises we make to one another. In doing so we choose to acknowledge the value of centrality, of organization, of community . . . it is our promises that hold us together.[2]

Other traditions that are creedal certainly make use of covenants as well. Ultimately, the very concept of covenant derives from the Hebrew Bible, in which the covenant expressed was that between God and God's people. Creedal traditions often draw upon that model to construct their covenants within their communities. Regardless of theology or tradition, covenants seek to be more than a manual for behavior, and are more an expression of faith in one another and how that faith lives out between and among us.

Covenants are meant to be living documents, revisited, revised, and retaught. The process usually begins with a community-wide conversation about what is important to the congregation to express. Again, we saw in the story of Irene's congregation in chapter 5 that a conversation about what is healthy helped reset the congregation's relationships after a difficult conflict. This is often when the need for covenant arises. The conversation is as important as the product for, as I've been saying all along, our culture does not often teach people healthy behavior, so these conversations become educational events as well. Then the task becomes how to make the covenant manifest in the day-to-day interactions in the congregation.

Some congregations integrate it into worship. This is most successful when covenants are short and poetic expressions. I've seen congregations use overly long and technical covenants in worship in a way that ends up alienating people from it. One parishioner in a church that did this said, "I feel like I'm being hit over the head with it, Sunday after Sunday!" I often say that covenants are made to be broken. I mean this to help people see that none of us is perfect and we inevitably make mistakes. If we behaved perfectly all the time, we would have no need for a covenant. But simply saying that does not avoid the problem of people still interpreting the covenant as punitive. Care must be taken in "enforcing" a covenant in a way that calls people back into a covenant, not a calling out that can humiliate. See again the worksheet in the appendix that Irene's church used to help people sort through their own feelings about a conflict they might be experiencing. It is a lovely way to remind people of the covenant without punishing them.

I often find covenants most useful when they are targeted to specific groups and specific purposes. Thinking about how particular guidelines relate to particular activities can help make a covenant much clearer and easier to apply. A colleague recently told me about a congregation that she served that was going through a major building campaign. In the beginning of the process, they developed a covenant that said, in essence: we covenant to be in right relationship to one another as much as we commit to the project itself. This served as a useful reminder when they got bogged down by disagreements about how to build what and where, that the real import of the building project was to help support the congregation, not to be a perfect building. And, that no one element of a building could be as important as the congregation's health.

Simone served an old historic church that was being confronted with a dreaded reality: should they renovate the antique house that had been used as a parsonage, which needed very expensive work? Or should they sell it and use the proceeds for other important parts of their ministry? The building had many historical and emotional connections, particularly for older members of the church, and they were loathe to let it go. From the beginning of their discussion process, Simone guided them in establishing a strict covenant for participating in the conversation. In order to speak, congregants had to first light a candle and say what they loved about the congregation. Only then could they state an opinion about the house. This helped remind each person, and the group collectively, that helping to sustain a loving congregation was more important than the details of what they were deciding. When the vote finally happened, the "winning" side did not clap or cheer. They all sat in the sanctuary and together sang a beloved hymn helping even those who had "lost" feel held in the larger whole. Incidentally, the vote was to sell the building, a decision that could easily have alienated many, but the process resulted in holding them together rather than driving them apart.

It must also be noted that care must be made in constructing covenants to be sensitive to cultural contexts and cultural nuances. Otherwise, they can unfortunately become tools of inadvertent harm, and can reinforce White hegemony. For example, in many White liberal congregations covenants often include such expectations as:

- Assume good intentions
- Speak with respect to others

Robin D'Angelo reflects on this in her book, *White Fragility*:

> The unexamined assumption underlying these guidelines is that they can be universally applied. But because they do not account for unequal power relations, they do not function the same way across race. These guidelines are primarily driven by white fragility, and they are accommodations made to coddle white fragility. The very conditions that most white people insist on to remain comfortable are those that support the racial status quo (white centrality, dominance, and professed innocence). For people of color, the racial status quo is hostile and needs to be interrupted, not reinforced. The essential message of trust is "be nice." And according to dominant white norms, the suggestion that someone is racist is not "nice."[3]

For example, if our covenant asks that we assume good intentions of one another, that reinforces the idea that our intentions trump our be-havior, thereby making it hard to call people to account for the harm they may do, even if they have good intentions. This critique has made me look again at how covenants can work in ways that may inadver-tently harm rather than heal.

Having said all this, I do believe there is still a place for the usefulness of covenants. If done well, they can actually help a group explore cultural difference, rather than enforcing cultural sameness. For example, if you have a group dedicated to difficult conversations about race and white supremacy, consider these guidelines from *Courageous Conversations*:

- Stay engaged: Staying engaged means remaining morally, emotionally, intellectually, and socially involved in the dialogue.
- Experience discomfort: This norm acknowledges that discomfort is inevitable, especially in dialogue about race, and that participants make a commitment to bring issues into the open.
- Speak your truth: This means being open about thoughts and feelings and not just saying what you think others want to hear.
- Expect and accept non-closure: This agreement asks participants to "hang out in uncertainty" and not rush to quick solutions, especially in relation to racial understanding, which requires ongoing dialogue.[4]

Understanding our congregations as covenantal communities is clearly central to our ability to work with conflict. If done with care, this can truly be transformational.

POLARITY MANAGEMENT

A tool that I find helpful in breaking people out of polarized, either/or thinking is one developed by Barry Johnson and described in his book, *Polarity Management*.[5] I have used this tool to work with congregations that are stuck and are trying to force people to choose sides. This process begins by first articulating the polarity that people are divided about. For the sake of this exercise, I'll take a fairly common one that emerges in mostly White congregations: whether to clap during music performances in worship. For some people, clapping completely disrupts their ability to lose themselves in the music. For others, it is a natural expression of joy and appreciation. We then start filling out a chart that looks like figure 9.1.

The upper quadrants are meant to describe all the positive reasons we would agree with one side of the polarity. Let's start with naming a few of the positives about clapping: it is a natural expression of appreciation; it allows for an embodied response; it taps into joy and freedom; it lets the participants feel a part of the music. It is helpful to have a group go through this exercise and participate in brainstorming what goes into each category. Thus, we see in figure 9.2 how this begins to get filled in.

Once we start to articulate the positive reactions to clapping, it begins to occur to us that there are negative aspects as well: clapping intrudes

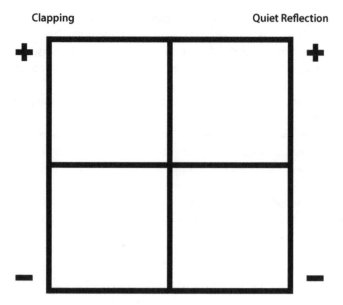

Figure 9.1. Polarity management (mostly blank). *Polarity diagrams developed by Barry Johnson.*

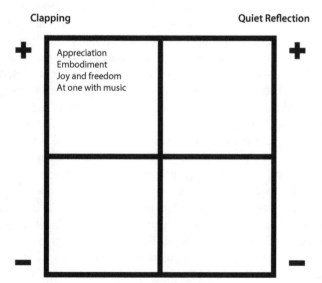

Figure 9.2. Polarity (upper-left quadrant filled in).

on a meditative feeling; it turns music into a performance, rather than an offering; if people only clap for some things and not others it could make the musicians feel unappreciated when there is no clapping (see figure 9.3). Again, engaging participants in naming these things is important.

Once we become hyper-aware of these negatives, we tend to then shoot up to the positives of the other pole, not clapping: it treats music as an offering; it allows people to have their meditative experience uninterrupted; it honors the solemnity of worship; it treats all musical offerings equally (figure 9.4).

And, yet again, we start to recognize the negatives of this pole: it can make worship feel stodgy and stilted; it doesn't allow for spontaneity of response; it privileges the head over the heart and body. And then we begin to start to feel the pull of the other pole (figure 9.5).

If we follow the movement of this progression, we can see where the lines lead us (figure 9.6): to the symbol of infinity!

And indeed, we begin to recognize that the fullness of life is found between and among the polarities. I am currently working with a music director who has found a brilliant solution to this argument: leadership! She indicates at the beginning of a meditative piece that this is one we might

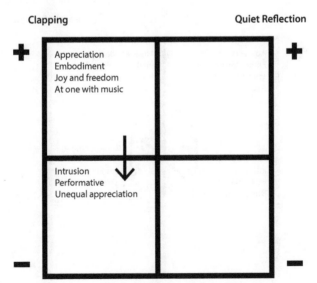

Figure 9.3. Polarity (upper- and lower-left quadrant filled in).

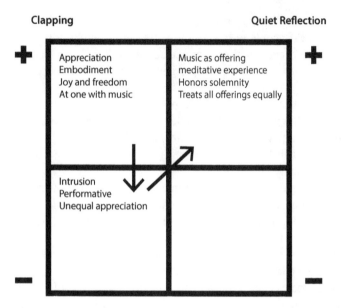

Figure 9.4. Polarity (upper- and lower-left and upper-right quadrant filled in).

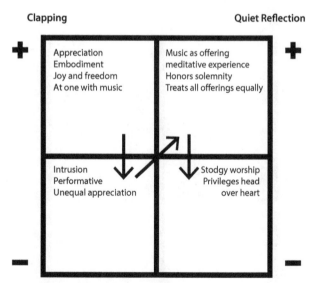

Figure 9.5. Polarity (all quadrants filled in).

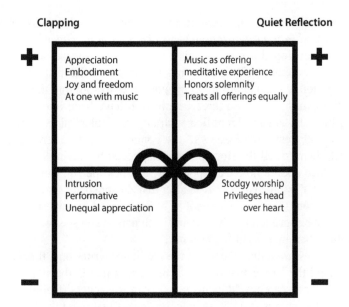

Figure 9.6. Polarity (infinity symbol superimposed).

prefer to appreciate in silence; or with a more rousing offering she will encourage clapping and movement. Both sides feel heard and appreciated with this simple intervention. Truth can indeed reside in both extremes.

When I have used this exercise, I am often surprised by how often the people who are most attached to one side or the other become really engaged with exploring the negative aspects of their own position! Somehow, exploring it this way takes the heat out of the issues, allowing people to feel heard without having to dig in, and opens them up to different ways of thinking about the issues. This process alone does not "resolve" the conflict, but it helps people relax out of their agitated states and start engaging in a creative exploration of complexity.

STORYTELLING

Margaret Benefiel, the executive director of the Shalem Institute for Spiritual Formation, introduced me to a powerful exercise by telling the story of a particularly charged experience in congregational or organizational life. Benefiel is the author of several notable books about spiritual leadership in organizations, including *The Soul at Work: Spiritual Leadership in Organizations*[6] and *The Soul of a Leader.*[7]

I have developed a form of this exercise to help tease out the elements of something significant that happened in the history of the congregation, the dynamics of which continues to spill into the present. It works like this: Choose three people who have been integral to the issue, but who are not identified with any particular "side," and who are also well-respected leaders of the congregation. In a large gathering, ask them to tell the story of what happened by having one person start: "Once upon a time, X happened." The next person can say, "But before that Y happened," or "And after that Z happened," and let it flow naturally from there. They are not to be interrupted by any observer. It should not be scripted in advance and each person can speak as they see fit, rather than in any particular order.

While they are telling the story, the facilitator writes on a flipchart or whiteboard the *values* that they hear being revealed in the story—such things as "transparency," "inclusivity," "care for others' feelings." The story usually comes to a natural conclusion. At that point the facilitator can ask the observers to review the list of values that were noted. They are then asked to identify a particular hymn or sacred text that seems to exemplify those values. Then everyone sings/reads it slowly together.

When I was first introduced to this, it sounded incredibly cheesy (to use a technical term!). But I have found it to be extremely powerful. There is something about concluding with a shared liturgical element that sacralizes the story. And in the storytelling and noting of the values, the participants get to hear the deeper intent of those involved. In essence, it is a way of creating an opportunity for everyone to walk down the ladder of their assumptions. I have also used this exercise with smaller groups that are stuck within a story as well. Harking back to the program I mentioned in chapter 2 in which Darden Smith developed in "Songwriting for Soldiers," we can see that the combination of storytelling and music can be deeply powerful in a subliminal way.

A ministerial association chose to make the dramatic step to professionalize the organization in a way that required new staffing and, of course, more money. Dues had to be raised substantially, which posed a challenge for many ministers who are not terribly well paid. While the association ultimately voted to affirm this plan, there were still difficult feelings about how it had been brought up and executed, particularly around the hiring of the new staff.

I was asked to facilitate a meeting between those who instituted the change and those who still were troubled by it. I utilized this story process so that the founding impetus and the values that lay within the decisions could be made clear. At the end of the process, a new sense of purpose and cohesion had emerged. By the time we sang a hymn together, there were tears in every eye. The disagreements didn't magically disappear. But the reminder of the unity of purpose helped sustain the group as it moved forward.

LISTENING CIRCLES

And now we come to one of the most powerful tools of all: listening circles. Many congregations have probably already had some experience with such circles as a way of doing spiritual exploration. In my tradition we often call them small-group ministry. They are conducted by trained facilitators (within the congregation) who help hold the group to a strict process of letting everyone speak of their own perspective or experience, with no interruptions, and sufficient space between each speaker to allow for deep listening. If you already have some kind of ministry like this you have a distinct advantage, because you already have a core group of people trained in facilitation. A much more detailed description of how to implement listening circles can be found in the *Little Book of Circle Processes.*[8]

In the context of conflict, listening circles allow for people to engage in dialogue rather than debate. They are designed to surface issues rather than to resolve them. They are inherently community-building experiences, because they create the opportunity for people to know each other more deeply. Sometimes they help people realize that perhaps they are the only one that has a particular perspective, which may help that person to let it go. Listening circles also are a way to include those least likely to participate in a larger public gathering, thereby gaining much-needed perspective from those who may be reluctant to publicly share and therefore are often not heard.

It is essential that you have a trained group of facilitators to lead these groups. They should be people who are not identified with strong positions about an issue. They should be able to hold people in a sacred space, which requires setting and holding appropriate boundaries. This requires a certain strength to withstand the inevitable pressure that will arise from the group to try to blur the boundaries.

Powerful questions are a key component of this process. You want to make sure that the questions you are giving people to talk about are as powerful as possible, allowing them to not get bogged down in assumptions but to hopefully engage in more creative conversation. It is important to take time to generate the questions and test for buried assumptions. As I talked about in the previous chapter, which introduced the concept, if the question is not truly powerful, it can undermine the process and contribute to frustration.

Groups of eight to ten people are ideal—any smaller and you don't get the range of perspectives that can be helpful, and any bigger will take too long to conduct the process. The facilitator begins by establishing a covenant with the group and making sure that all agree to its conditions. This covenant needs to include the important component of not allowing cross-talk or interruptions. Confidentiality should be requested in this particular sense: it will be inevitable that people will want to share some of the ideas that they heard in the circle, ideas that were illuminating for them. But they should not relate *who* shared the idea in the circle. The timing of these groups should be limited to a total of three hours, including a break.

If you are using these groups to learn more about where people stand on a particular issue, you can ask for someone in the group to record the responses in paraphrased form; again, not attributed to any particular person. The combined set of responses from all the groups can then be used by your leadership to better understand what the wider congregation is thinking about. It is best to then summarize these responses in the newsletter or some other vehicle so that there is transparency to the process.

A seminary that began as one serving a fairly conservative denomination had recently started admitting students from other, more liberal traditions. This began as a way of addressing reduced enrollment and therefore reduced resources. But the leadership of the seminary also hoped that the interchange among perspectives could be helpful to all. The students were not so sure about that. Those that came from conservative backgrounds were troubled by many of the liberal perspectives that they were hearing—perspectives they had been taught to see as dangerous. The liberal students felt disturbed by the conservative positions that they felt forced to hear, that they always felt to be constricting. The fractures in the community were becoming problematic and erupting into classrooms and other interactions as well.

A facilitator came in to work with them and suggested listening circles as a process for everyone to hear each other. The leadership generated what they hoped was a powerful question: "How might we learn together as a diverse and dynamic community without undermining individual perspectives?" What happened in the groups was powerful for almost everyone. They learned that each "side" felt silenced and misunderstood. Their sympathy for one another was activated, and they began to understand that their learning could help strengthen their faith by exploring challenges to it.

The result of listening circles may not be to come to a big decision about something people are conflicted about. Sometimes they simply serve the purpose, as described above, of helping people understand one another better.

Listening circles take time: time to train the facilitators, time to develop the questions, time to organize the groups, time to allow the groups to meet on their own schedule. This length of process can be frustrating to some. But allowing the time can also help lower the anxiety and let go of the sense of counterproductive urgency. It is important to explain the steps of these processes from the beginning to the congregation so that members can understand why and how the processes will be done, and what you hope to gain from going through them.

A congregation that I worked with first began using listening circles during a time of high conflict. They found them so helpful that they started using them on a regular basis, at least twice a year, just to check in with people about the ministry and how things are going. This practice helped inevitable conflicts be aired without letting them go underground or resulting in polarization. Participants found them to be not only community-building experiences, but also faith-building experiences, as they were able to see how one another lived their faith in the world.

A PLAN OF ACTION

So now that I have thrown out this multitude of strategies, I imagine you are wondering which of them to use and when!

The first place to start if you have a difficult conflict popping up is to take a deep breath. As I have been saying, a false sense of urgency can be counterproductive. Just because something is *important* doesn't mean it needs to be *immediate.* And immediate action is almost guaranteed to be a reaction, chock-full of anxiety. Try to hold your leadership body in a place of nonreactivity, as much as possible. Utilizing the process of learning to ask powerful questions about the difficult issues can help everyone test their assumptions and create a larger frame of perspective.

On a personal level, just as I talked about earlier in the book, it is essential that you do the work of understanding your place in the conflict: What is it bringing up in you? How do you manage your own anxiety? What do you need to take responsibility for? Utilize the worksheet in the appendix to try to surface your own feelings and concerns. Ask for perspective from friends or family, therapists, or coaches. Without going through this important process, you risk sabotaging—even if unconsciously—whatever larger process the congregation may be engaging in.

At any point in a conflict, whether latent or exploding, it is important to start the work of helping teach as many people as possible about healthy responses to conflict. This book is designed for that very purpose, so that you need not be a conflict expert to help the congregation begin to engage with this learning. I have often been called in to help a congregation address a conflict, with their clear expectation that I will help them to "fix" it. Instead of doing so, I immediately start training the leadership body in developing their own conflict skills. I am often surprised at how this helps to take the urgency out of the situation and creates an attitude of reflection and growth, and starts to build their confidence that they can actually do this work themselves.

If the issues are of concern to the majority of the congregation, begin to undertake the process of utilizing listening circles. As I said, this takes time, which can sometimes dissipate anxiety. Though you must be prepared for the frustration that length of time will inevitably produce, helping people understand the goals of the process can help mitigate against this.

Some of these other tools can be used as the situation calls for. A particularly polarized issue can benefit from engaging in a polarity management exercise. A lingering major issue in the congregation's past or present can be helped by a storytelling exercise.

The most important strategy of all is to ask for help. Utilize middle judicatories, denominational resources, consultants, and coaches. It is incredibly difficult to gain perspective on your situation only from within your system.

Most of all, know that you really do have the capacity to do this work. Oftentimes when we are physically ill, it can feel like we will never get better. Similarly, when in the midst of a painful conflict, it is easy to get lost in despair when you are in the throes of something so difficult. One of the great pleasures of the work I did as a district executive was to see congregations grow and change over time. The congregation I mentioned early in this book that used to welcome people by saying, "Welcome to our church, we hate our minister!" finally went through a deeply introspective process that resulted in calling a healthy minister that is still serving them well 15 years later. Things do get better! Have faith in yourself and your people.

Questions for Discussion:

- Which of the tools introduced here might be useful to try in your congregation right now?
- Have there been processes that you have tried that have failed, and can you discern why?
- How might you begin to develop a plan for training your congregation in healthy conflict behavior?

Chapter Ten

The Courage of
Creative Imagination

Where did we nourish and foster the creative imagination that permits you to bring into the world something that does not now exist? That's the real challenge of a lot of the work of conflict, is that you're trying to bring something that does not now exist. That's the creative act.

—John Paul Lederach[1]

The challenge of our time is to mobilize great masses of people to make change without dehumanizing one another. Not just because it's morally right but because it works. Lasting change, the kind that seeps into people's hearts, has only ever come about through a combination of pressure and good conflict. Both matter.

—Amanda Ripley[2]

In *High Conflict: Why We Get Trapped and How We Get Out*, Amanda Ripley tells a story about Gary Friedman, a pioneer in the art of conflict mediation. Gary had become famous in his professional life as one of the premier practitioners of mediation, but he found himself embroiled in a high-conflict situation within his community. A friend had asked him to run for office to serve on a volunteer community board. He was in his retirement years, and looking for a way to utilize his skills that didn't involve constant travel and stress. He agreed to do it, because he felt like the community was being stultified by an "old guard," and he thought he knew how to create change. Almost immediately Gary

began to lose himself in "us and them" politics, and he exerted his considerable popularity to become chair of the board, so that he could beat
back what he considered the opposition. Gary started to completely lose
sight of everything that he had ever understood or taught about conflict.
He was stuck in what Ripley calls the "tarpits" of high conflict.

Gary could hardly recognize himself, and his family and friends
certainly did not. He was high-handed in meetings, refusing to give
people a chance to fully express themselves. He said and wrote deroga-
tory things about the "old guard" that elevated the conflict even further.
The opposition began to organize and announced that they were going
to vote him out of office. He decided to call a special meeting to call
out these folks, but then he suddenly realized what was happening and
asked himself,

> "Who am I really calling the special meeting for?" And he had to admit
> he was calling it for himself, for his own need to feel right and feel good.
>   So he paused. He repeated a mantra he sometimes used on himself: "I
> am not important, and this is not important."[3]

He began to realize how far he had fallen, and called this period a time
of recovery from his "personal derangement":

> There was a new complexity in his language. He was "holding the ten-
> sion," as he put it. Not collapsing into good versus evil, us versus them.
> He'd carved out enough space for complexity in his own mind. And this
> meant he was seeing the world more accurately, in full.[4]

Gary decided to stay on the board, but nominated a new chair himself, so people could see that he was moving in a different direction. He
finally remembered his mediation skills and began to help neighbors
understand each other's concerns. He learned to ask himself some important questions: "*Does it need to be said?* If the answer was yes, then
he'd ask himself: *Does it need to be said by me?* And if still yes: *Does it
need to be said by me right now?* It was surprising how often the answer
was no."[5] He started initiating simple interactions and conversations,
outside of any political concerns, which helped him reconnect to his
community in an important way. As Ripley notes,

> These interactions are small inoculations, which, taken regularly, protect
> us from making the errors in judgment and interpretation that can lead to

high conflict. Psychologists Julie and John Goodman have studied conflict in some three thousand married couples over the years, and they've
found that the couples most capable of keeping conflict healthy were the
ones whose everyday positive interactions exceeded the negative by a
ratio of 5 to 1. This is the "magic ratio," as they put it. . . .

When sixty-five men who had spent the winter together at Antarctic
research stations were asked about what had unified them, 40 percent
mentioned the importance of singing and playing games together. It was
the single most unifying factor.

I relate this story at some length because it brings together so many
of the themes of this book. After getting completely stuck in his amygdala for reasons mysterious even to himself, Gary was able to utilize
the art of self-reflection to break the spell. Rather than being consumed
with changing the system, he changed himself and his own behavior,
which, ironically, changed the system. He was able to reconnect to his
community in a new and different way, and hold the space for others
to learn how to work with conflict in a better way as well. As Ripley
says, "The challenge of our time is to mobilize great masses of people to
make change without dehumanizing one another. Not just because it's
morally right but because it works."[6] This work of transforming conflict
is not just high-minded, it is also eminently practical.

Isn't this exactly what we are trying to create in our religious communities: a space in which a person can find themselves anew, in which
they can reconnect with a loving community, and help everyone learn
a new way of being. And religious communities are *exactly* the kinds
of places where the "magic ratio" of human connection can take place,
thereby changing the person, the community, and, I believe, the world.
Transformation.

We hear about transformation all the time now. And indeed, our
world is in need of transformation at so many levels: we need to transform our understanding of our relationship to the earth from one of
exploitation to one of interconnection; we need to transform our understanding of racism from something that existed in the past to something
that pervades our whole culture, whether conscious or not. You've been
hearing about transformation throughout this book. It can often seem
that we talk about transformation as if it were easy. And, of course,
it is not! As we see in the story above, transformation requires us to
disengage with how we've been doing things, before we even really

know how to engage with a new way. Who would willingly do this if they didn't have to? Conflict forces us to do so, and, startingly, we become better people because of it.

As I said earlier in the book, we really don't have a choice about whether we engage with adaptive challenges or not: they are what we are facing. But simply saying "we have to" does not exactly motivate us to make the scary and necessary changes. For me, the answer to the challenge of why we should do this is: *because this is where creativity lies.* We don't have the ability to completely *make* our future, but we do have the ability to *imagine* it, which is a necessary step for transformation.

Glennon Doyle, the wildly popular memoirist and activist, has inspired an entire generation of women to *reimagine* their lives. Rather than continuing to accept the scripts we were given as our younger selves, she encourages us to take the risk and let go into the unknown. "Courage is the presence of fear, and going anyway,"[7] she encourages. "There is a life meant for you that is truer than the one you're living. But in order to have it, you will have to forge it yourself. You will have to create on the outside what you are imagining on the inside. Only you can bring it forth. And it will cost you everything."[8] That hardly makes it sound easy! But I think the reason she is so inspiring to millions of people is that she constantly asks them to think about "What is the truest, most beautiful story about your life you can imagine?"[9]

It is hard work to break out of the constrictions of highly amygdalated states of conflict. But the promise of doing so is the freedom on the other side: the freedom to create a new story, together.

One of my early ministries was rife with conflict: some of which was endemic to the system, and some of which I certainly contributed to. I was determined to wait out the worst of it so that I didn't feel like I had been driven out. And I did. I left as things were finally calming down. But I left without a new story. I left without having contributed to building a new story of a new way of doing things in that old, stuck system. That is where fear took me. It was soul-destroying.

The experience I described in an earlier chapter about allowing a group to come to a creative place, without my control or interference, was a life-giving experience. We were able to create a new story together—one that many people believed could never be told. And I learned to repeat that formula again and again: let go and learn.

I have thought again and again over the years about how I could have handled my previous difficulties in a healthier way. I've learned a lot from this cogitation. But it is negative learning. What I have found in the work of conflict transformation is the opportunity to learn in an ongoing, open, and creative way. That doesn't mean that it is always easy. Far from it. But instead of opting to walk away as I did in the past, I now try to work past my fears and resistance and old traumas toward a new way of being.

Sometimes for the sake of our health and well-being we must walk away. Every conflict is not necessarily transformable. But often we have a chance to walk toward new life, a new story, an emboldened soul. Our religious communities are one of the only places in our current culture where we can find and embrace this new life, held and emboldened by our faith and one another.

I hope that in the pages of this book I've given you some new ways of looking at conflict, some insights about your past, and some tools for your future. They do not promise a perfect, conflict-free life. More the opposite. They hopefully give you a way of working with the inevitable conflicts in your life as important experiences of learning and change. I do believe they can help move all of us forward in life-affirming and healing ways. And I can testify that these tools, when used well, do indeed work in congregations, and help move them forward into greater health and vitality.

I continue to make mistakes in this work. Some pieces of it I have to learn over and over again. But I have found that walking on this path has led me to a closer sense of what I believe God wants for me: the fullest expression of all that I and the communities I serve can be. This, alone, is motivation to keep walking.

Appendix
Conflict Processing Worksheet

**HEALTHY CONGREGATION TEAM, FOX VALLEY
UNITARIAN UNIVERSALIST FELLOWSHIP**

Think of a conflict you are in, or have been in.

1. Briefly describe the situation.

2. What is your relationship to the people involved?

3. What are your feelings?

4. In what way does the conflict affect you personally?

5. In what ways does the conflict affect the broader situation?

6. Are these relationships you care about?

7. Will the situation matter a month from now?

8. Can I change the situation?

Summary:

- If you don't have strong feelings about the relationships involved or if it is not an important situation: *You may want to consider letting go, moving on.*
- If you do have strong feelings or the situation impacts important issues: *You may want to consider some ways of resolving the issue.*

Reframing the Problem

1. How have you tried to deal with this conflict?

2. What common ground do you have with the other person(s)? Is there another way to achieve common goals?

3. What experiences or situations from the past does this situation recall for you?

4. What will happen if the situation doesn't get resolved?

5. Are you willing at this point to make these statements?
   - I can make this conflict situation better.
     ☐Yes
     ☐No
   - I want to make it better.
     ☐Yes
     ☐No
   - I am willing to try something new.
     ☐Yes
     ☐No

Summary:

- If you answered NO to the statements in question 5, you might want to take some more time to think about the situation.
- If you answered YES to the statements in question 5, you might want to explore some possible solutions.

Possible Solutions

What would it look like if the situation were better? List some things you could do to make it better:

1.

2.

3.

Of the things you could try, which are the ones you are most willing to do?

Notes

INTRODUCTION

1. Sarah Schulman, *Conflict Is Not Abuse: Overstating Harm, Community Responsibility and the Duty of Repair* (Vancouver, BC: Arsenal Pulp Press, 2016), 16–17.

CHAPTER ONE

1. John Paul Lederach, *Reconcile: Conflict Transformation for Ordinary Christians* (Harrisonburg, VA: Herald Press, 2014), preface.

2. Ibid.

3. F. Scott Fitzgerald, "The Crack-Up," *Esquire,* February 1936.

4. John Paul Lederach, *The Little Book of Conflict Transformation* (New York: Good Books, 2003), 14.

5. Lederach, *Reconcile,* preface.

6. Gilbert R. Rendle, personal conversation.

7. Gilbert R. Rendle, *Quietly Courageous: Leading the Church in a Changing World* (Lanham, MD: Rowman & Littlefield, 2018), 12–13.

8. Susan Beaumont, *How to Lead When You Don't Know Where You're Going* (Lanham, MD: Rowman & Littlefield, 2019), 1.

9. William Bridges, *Transitions: Making Sense of Life's Changes* (Boston: De Capo Books, 2004), xii.

10. Richard Rohr, *Everything Belongs: The Gift of Contemplative Prayer* (New York: Crossroad Publishing, 1999), 155–56.

11. adrienne maree brown, *We Will Not Cancel Us* (Chico, CA: AK Press, 2020), 6.

12. Ibid., 7.

CHAPTER TWO

1. Resmaa Menakem, *My Grandmother's Hands* (Las Vegas, NV: Central Recovery Press, 2018), 12.

2. Ibid.

3. Louis Cozolino, *The Neuroscience of Psychotherapy*, third edition (New York: W. W. Norton & Company, 2017).

4. Ibid., 178.

5. Mario Mikulincer and Phillip R. Shaver, *Attachment in Adulthood*, second edition (New York: Guilford Press, 2016).

6. Ibid., 59.

7. Martha Henriques, "Can the Legacy of Trauma Be Passed Down the Generations?" *BBC Future*, March 26, 2019, https://www.bbc.com/future/article/20190326-what-is-epigenetics.

8. Menakem, *My Grandmother's Hands*, 294.

9. Ibid., 13.

10. David Conrads, "Darden Smith Listens, Strums a Bit, Then Helps Soldiers Write Their Song," *Christian Science Monitor*, June 13, 2014.

11. Ibid.

12. Ibid.

13. Iain McGilchrist, *The Divided Brain and the Search for Meaning* (New Haven, CT: Yale University Press, 2012), Kindle edition.

14. Ibid., location 124–35.

15. From Chris Argyris, *Overcoming Organizational Defenses: Facilitating Organizational Learning*, first edition (Upper Saddle River, NJ: Pearson, 1990).

CHAPTER THREE

1. Brené Brown, *Braving the Wilderness* (New York: Random House, 2017), 157.

2. The work of Mario Mikulincer and Phillip R. Shaver, *Attachment in Adulthood*, second edition (Guilford Press, 2016), referenced in the previous chapter, offers helpful strategies for working through our attachment systems.

3. Brown, *Braving the Wilderness*, 157.

4. Jenny Smith, "The Second Marathon: A Thought for Pastors on Walking the New Normal," *Jennie Smith* (blog), July 2, 2021, https://www.jenny smithwrites.com/post/the-second-marathon-a-word-for-pastors-on-walking -the-new-normal.

5. Jenny Smith, *Your Palms Up Life* (email newsletter), https://jenniferkay smith.us19.list-manage.com/subscribe?u=c5c88ec6c9365796292154bb6&id =87237965da.

6. Resmaa Menakem, *My Grandmother's Hands* (Las Vegas, NV: Central Recovery Press, 2018), 5.

7. David Whyte, *Consolations: The Solace, Nourishment and Underlying Meaning of Everyday Words* (Langley, WA: Many Rivers Press, 2015), 21–22.

8. See the work of Edwin Friedman and Peter Steinke (see the bibliography) in particular.

9. Jack Shitama, *Anxious Church, Anxious People* (Earlesville, MD: Charis Works, 2018), 22.

10. Brown, *Braving the Wilderness*, 31.

11. Ibid., 149–50.

12. Recommended authors of work on the Enneagram to explore: Richard Rohr, Russ Hudson, Don Richard Riso, Ian Morgan Cron, and Helen Palmer.

13. William Ury, *The Power of a Positive No* (New York: Bantam Books, 2007).

14. Roger Fisher and William Ury, *Getting to Yes* (Boston: Houghton, Mifflin, Harcourt, 1981).

15. Whyte, *Consolations*, 21.

CHAPTER FOUR

1. Quoted in Brené Brown, *Braving the Wilderness* (New York: Random House, 2017), 132.

2. Richard Rohr, "Daily Meditation," Center for Action and Contemplation, March 2, 2021, https://cac.org/confirmation-bias-2021-03-02/.

3. Jacqui Lewis, "Why Can't We See?" (podcast), as quoted in Rohr, "Daily Meditation."

4. Quoted in Brown, *Braving the Wilderness*, 132.

5. Kendra Cherry, "What Is the Negativity Bias?" verywellmind.com, April 29, 2020, https://www.verywellmind.com/negative-bias-4589618.

6. Amanda Ripley, *High Conflict: Why We Get Trapped and How We Get Out* (New York: Simon and Schuster, 2021), 5–6.

CHAPTER FIVE

1. Lynn Ungar, "Weaving," from *Breathe* (self-published, 2020), 30.
2. Gilbert R. Rendle, *The Multigenerational Congregation* (Washington DC: Alban Institute, 2002).
3. Gary Peluso-Verdend, *Paying Attention: Focusing Your Congregation on What Matters* (Washington, DC: Alban Institute, 2005).
4. Ibid., 11.
5. Gilbert R. Rendle, *Quietly Courageous: Leading the Church in a Changing World* (Lanham, MD: Rowman & Littlefield, 2018), 165–66.
6. From John Paul Lederach, *Preparing for Peace: Conflict Transformation across Cultures* (Syracuse, NY: Syracuse University Press, 1995).
7. David Brubaker, "Congregational Constants," Congregational Consulting Group, May 3, 2021, https://www.congregationalconsulting.org/congregational -constants/.

CHAPTER SIX

1. Victoria Safford, "The Sacraments of Word and Celebration," in John Millspaugh (ed.), *A People So Bold* (Boston: Skinner House, 2010), Kindle edition, location 1470.
2. Robin Hammeal-Urban, *Wholeness after Betrayal* (New York: Morehouse Publishing, 2015), Kindle edition, location 308–15.
3. Deborah J. Pope-Lance, "Congregations with a History of Misconduct," in Barbara Child and Keith Kron (eds.), *In the Interim* (Boston: Skinner House, 2017), Kindle edition, location 3309–15.
4. Safford, "The Sacraments of Word and Celebration," location 1470.

CHAPTER SEVEN

1. See especially Robin D'Angelo, *White Fragility* (Boston: Beacon Press, 2018).
2. Resmaa Menakem, *My Grandmother's Hands* (Las Vegas, NV: Central Recovery Press, 2018), 11.
3. Ibid., 12.
4. Jonathan M. Pitts, "In Slavery, Her Family Was Owned by His. Now They Attend a Baltimore Church Seeking to Atone for Its Past," *Baltimore Sun*, September 12, 2019, https://www.baltimoresun.com/maryland/baltimore-city /bs-md-ci-church-slavery-atonement-20190912-3tllerewzzh7nnqsa5entffssy -story.html.

5. Ibid.

6. Jonathan M. Pitts, "Episcopal Church Established by Baltimore Slave Owners Creates $500,000 Reparations Fund," *Baltimore Sun*, January 29, 2021, https://www.baltimoresun.com/maryland/baltimore-city/bs-md-church -reparations-20210129-jmiroxmrarc37a54ykonanoc2y-story.html.

7. Pitts, "In Slavery . . . "

8. Ibid.

9. Ibid.

CHAPTER EIGHT

1. Gilbert R. Rendle, *Quietly Courageous: Leading the Church in a Changing World* (Lanham, MD: Rowman & Littlefield, 2018), 231–32.

2. Ibid., 228–29.

3. Ron Heifetz, Alexander Grashow, and Marty Linski, *The Practice of Adaptive Leadership* (Cambridge, MA: Harvard Business School Press, 2009).

4. Rendle, *Quietly Courageous*, 232.

5. Heifetz et al., *The Practice of Adaptive Leadership*, 7–8.

6. Ibid., 28–29.

7. Eric Vogt, Juanita Brown, and David Isaacs, *The Art and Architecture of Powerful Questions* (Mill Valley, CA: Whole Systems Associates, 2003), 4, https://www.sparc.bc.ca/wp-content/uploads/2020/11/the-art-of-powerful -questions.pdf.

8. adrienne maree brown, *Holding Change* (Chico, CA: AK Press, 2021), 149.

9. Kenneth Jones and Tema Okun, "Dismantling Racism: A Workbook for Social Change Groups," Changework, 2001, http://www.cwsworkshop.org /PARC_site_B/dr-culture.html.

10. Ibid.

11. Jenny Smith, "Blow Up the Damn Pedestal: An Open Letter to Pastors," *Jenny Smith* (blog), August 19, 2020, https://www.jennysmithwrites.com/post /blow-up-the-damn-pedestal-an-open-letter-to-pastors.

CHAPTER NINE

1. Gerald May, Will and Spirit (HarperCollins, 2009) Location 41, ebook.

2. Report of the UUA Commission on Appraisal, *Unlocking the Power of Covenant* (Boston: Unitarian Universalist Association, 2021), 68.

3. Robin D'Angelo, *White Fragility* (Boston: Beacon Press, 2018), 128.

4. Adapted from Glenn E. Singleton and Curtis Linton, *Courageous Conversations about Race* (Thousand Oaks, CA: Corwin Press, 2006), 58–65.

5. Barry Johnson, *Polarity Management* (Amherst, MA: HRD Press, 1996).

6. Margaret Benefiel, *Soul at Work: Spiritual Leadership in Organizations* (New York: Seabury Books, 2005).

7. Margaret Benefiel, *The Soul of a Leader* (Chestnut Ridge, NY: Crossroads Books, 2008).

8. Kay Pranis, *The Little Book of Circle Processes* (New York: Good Books, 2005).

CHAPTER TEN

1. John Paul Lederach, "The Ingredients of Social Courage," interview with Krista Tippett, *On Being*, June 7, 2018 (transcript: https://onbeing.org/programs/america-ferrera-john-paul-lederach-the-ingredients-of-social-courage/).

2. Amanda Ripley, *High Conflict: Why We Get Trapped and How We Get Out* (New York: Simon and Schuster, 2021), 13.

3. Ibid., 204.

4. Ibid, 200.

5. Ibid., 201.

6. Ibid., 13.

7. Glennon Doyle, "Courage Is the Presence of Fear," interview with Krista Tippett, *On Being*, January 24, 2019 (transcript: https://onbeing.org/programs/glennon-doyle-and-abby-wambach-courage-is-the-presence-of-fear-and-going-anyway/).

8. Glennon Doyle, *Untamed* (New York, Random House, 2020), 52.

9. Ibid., 68.

Bibliography

Argyris, Chris. *Overcoming Organizational Defenses: Facilitating Organizational Learning*, first edition. Upper Saddle River, NJ: Pearson, 1990.

Beaumont, Susan. *How to Lead When You Don't Know Where You're Going.* Lanham, MD: Rowman & Littlefield, 2019.

Benefiel, Margaret. *Soul at Work: Spiritual Leadership in Organizations.* New York: Seabury Books, 2005.

Benefiel, Margaret. *The Soul of a Leader.* Chestnut Ridge, NY: Crossroads Books, 2008.

Bridges, William. *Transitions: Making Sense of Life's Changes.* Boston, MA: Da Capo Books, 2004.

brown, adrienne maree. *Holding Change.* Chico, CA: AK Press, 2021.

brown, adrienne maree. *We Will Not Cancel Us.* Chico, CA: AK Press, 2020.

Brown, Brené. *Braving the Wilderness.* New York: Random House, 2017.

Brubaker, David. "Congregational Constants." Congregational Consulting Group, May 3, 2021. https://www.congregationalconsulting.org/congregational-constants/.

Cherry, Kendra. "What Is the Negativity Bias?" verywellmind.com, April 29, 2020. https://www.verywellmind.com/negative-bias-4589618.

Conrads, David. "Darden Smith Listens, Strums a Bit, Then Helps Soldiers Write Their Song." *Christian Science Monitor*, June 13, 2014.

Cozolino, Louis. *The Neuroscience of Psychotherapy*, third edition. New York: W. W. Norton & Company, 2017.

D'Angelo, Robin. *White Fragility.* Boston: Beacon Press, 2018.

Doyle, Glennon. "Courage Is the Presence of Fear." Interview with Krista Tippet, *On Being*, January 24, 2019. https://onbeing.org/programs/glennon

-doyle-and-abby-wambach-courage-is-the-presence-of-fear-and-going-any way/.

Doyle, Glennon. *Untamed.* New York: Random House, 2020.

Fisher, Roger, and William Ury. *Getting to Yes.* Boston: Houghton Mifflin Harcourt, 1981.

Fitzgerald, F. Scott. "The Crack-Up." *Esquire,* February 1936.

Friedman, Edwin H. *A Failure of Nerve: Leadership in the Age of the Quick Fix.* New York: Seabury Press, 2007.

Hammeal-Urban, Robin. *Wholeness after Betrayal.* New York: Morehouse Publishing, 2015.

Heifetz, Ron, Alexander Grashow, and Marty Linski. *The Practice of Adaptive Leadership.* Cambridge, MA: Harvard Business School Press, 2009.

Henriques, Martha. "Can the Legacy of Trauma Be Passed Down the Generations?" *BBC Future,* March 26, 2019. https://www.bbc.com/future /article/20190326-what-is-epigenetics.

Johnson, Barry. *Polarity Management.* Amherst, MA: HRD Press, 1996.

Jones, Kenneth, and Tema Okun. "Dismantling Racism: A Workbook for Social Change Groups. Changework, 2001. http://www.cwsworkshop.org /PARC_site_B/dr-culture.html.

Lederach, John Paul. "The Ingredients of Social Courage." Interview with Krista Tippet, *On Being,* June 7, 2018. https://onbeing.org/programs/america -ferrera-john-paul-lederach-the-ingredients-of-social-courage/.

Lederach, John Paul. *The Little Book of Conflict Transformation.* New York: Good Books, 2003.

Lederach, John Paul. *Preparing for Peace: Conflict Transformation across Cultures.* Syracuse, NY: Syracuse University Press, 1995.

Lederach, John Paul. *Reconcile: Conflict Transformation for Ordinary Christians.* Harrisonburg, VA: Herald Press, 2014.

May, Gerald. *Will and Spirit.* New York, NY: HarperCollins, 2009.

McGilchrist, Iain. *The Divided Brain and the Search for Meaning.* New Haven, CT: Yale University Press, 2012.

Menakem, Resmaa. *My Grandmother's Hands.* Las Vegas, NV: Central Recovery Press, 2018.

Mikulincer, Mario, and Phillip R. Shaver. *Attachment in Adulthood,* second edition. New York: Guilford Press, 2016.

Peluso-Verdend, Gary. *Paying Attention: Focusing Your Congregation on What Matters.* Washington, DC: Alban Institute, 2005.

Pitts, Jonathan M. "Episcopal Church Established by Baltimore Slave Owners Creates $500,000 Reparations Fund." *Baltimore Sun,* January 29, 2021. https://www.baltimoresun.com/maryland/baltimore-city/bs-md-church-re parations-20210129-jmiroxmrarc37a54ykonanoc2y-story.html.

Pitts, Jonathan M. "In Slavery, Her Family Was Owned by His. Now They Attend a Baltimore Church Seeking to Atone for Its Past." *Baltimore Sun*, September 12, 2019. https://www.baltimoresun.com/maryland/baltimore -city/bs-md-ci-church-slavery-atonement-20190912-3tllerewzzh7nnqsa5ent ffssy-story.html.

Pope-Lance, Deborah J. "Congregations with a History of Misconduct." In *In the Interim*, edited by Barbara Child and Keith Kron. Boston: Skinner House, 2017.

Pranis, Kay. *The Little Book of Circle Processes*. New York: Good Books, 2005.

Rendle, Gilbert R. *The Multigenerational Congregation*. Washington DC: Alban Institute, 2002.

Rendle, Gilbert R. *Quietly Courageous: Leading the Church in a Changing World*. Lanham, MD: Rowman & Littlefield, 2018.

Ripley, Amanda. *High Conflict: Why We Get Trapped and How We Get Out*. New York: Simon and Schuster, 2021.

Rohr, Richard. "Daily Meditation." Center for Action and Contemplation, March 2, 2021. https://cac.org/jesus-and-bias-2021-03-03/.

Rohr, Richard. *Everything Belongs: The Gift of Contemplative Prayer*. New York: Crossroad Publishing, 1999.

Safford, Victoria. "The Sacraments of Word and Celebration." In *A People So Bold*, edited by John Millspaugh. Boston: Skinner House, 2010.

Schulman, Sarah. *Conflict Is Not Abuse: Overstating Harm, Community Responsibility and the Duty of Repair*. Vancouver, BC: Arsenal Pulp Press, 2016.

Shitama, Jack. *Anxious Church, Anxious People*. Earlesville, MD: Charis Works, 2018.

Singleton, Glenn E., and Curtis Linton. *Courageous Conversations about Race*. Thousand Oaks, CA: Corwin Press, 2006.

Smith, Jenny. "Blow Up the Damn Pedestal: An Open Letter to Pastors." *Jenny Smith* (blog), August 19, 2020. https://www.jennysmithwrites.com/post /blow-up-the-damn-pedestal-an-open-letter-to-pastors.

Smith, Jenny. "The Second Marathon: A Thought for Pastors on Walking the New Normal." *Jennie Smith* (blog), July 2, 2021. https://www.jennysmith writes.com/post/the-second-marathon-a-word-for-pastors-on-walking-the -new-normal.

Smith, Jenny. *Your Palms Up Life*. https://jenniferkaysmith.us19.list-manage .com/subscribe?u=c5c88ec6c9365796292154bb6&id=87237965da.

Steinke, Peter. *Congregational Leadership in Anxious Times*. Washington DC: Alban Institute, 2006.

Ungar, Lynn. *Breathe*. Self-published, 2020.

Ury, William. *The Power of a Positive No*. New York: Bantam Books, 2007.

UUA Commission on Appraisal. *Unlocking the Power of Covenant.* Boston: Unitarian Universalist Association, 2021.

Vogt, Eric, Juanita Brown, and David Isaacs. *The Art and Architecture of Powerful Questions.* Mill Valley, CA: Whole Systems Associates, 2003. https://www.sparc.bc.ca/wp-content/uploads/2020/11/the-art-of-powerful-questions.pdf.

Whyte, David. *Consolations: The Solace, Nourishment and Underlying Meaning of Everyday Words.* Langley, WA: Many Rivers Press, 2015.

Index

About the Author

Terasa Cooley has served over 30 years as a parish minister and denominational official. Ordained as a Unitarian Universalist, she has served congregations in Detroit; Chicago; Hartford, Connecticut; Arlington, Virginia; and Pasadena, California. In her denominational service she provided resources and training for congregations in the Boston area, and created national programs on healthy congregational functioning in subsequent roles. She is a renowned speaker and trainer on issues of congregational conflict, adaptive leadership, strategic planning, and entrepreneurial ministries. A native of Texas, Cooley received her Bachelor of Arts degree in English literature from the University of Texas, her Master of Divinity from Harvard Divinity School, and her Doctor of Ministry from Hartford Seminary. She is an accredited interim minister specializing in congregations recovering from conflict and misconduct.

Printed in the USA
CPSIA information can be obtained
at www.ICGtesting.com
LVHW051632180324
774809LV00009B/156